COACHING
THE DEFENSIVE SECONDARY:

BY THE EXPERTS

Edited by
Earl Browning

ISBN: 1-58518-308-3

Library of Congress Catalog Card Number: 00-105370

Cover Design: Jennifer Bokelmann

Developmental Editor: Kim Heusel

Page Layout: Kim Heusel

Coaches Choice

P.O. Box 1828

Monterey, CA 93942

www.coacheschoiceweb.com

Table of Contents

Chapter 1

ZONE PASS DEFENSIVE TECHNIQUES

Ron Cooper
Eastern Michigan University
1993

There are some basic requirements for all linebackers and defensive backs. We tell our backs these things must happen. The first thing we discuss is *attitude.* It is the most important. Second is *pride.* We want them to be the best at their job. Third is *confidence.* They must believe in themselves. Next is *poise.* They must always be in control. Then comes *aggressiveness.* We want them to break on the ball, increase interception distance, and hit people. The last requirement is *preparation.*

We list our objectives. Let me give you our list so you can see what we are trying to accomplish.

1. Be 100 percent fundamentally sound.

2. No bombs; run or pass.

3. No mental errors or missed assignments.

4. Make interceptions; force turnovers.

5. Disrupt by disguise.

6. No missed tackles.

7. Play together.

We put in the game plan on Monday. We work on it on Tuesday and Wednesday. We polish it on Thursday. We get ready to play on Saturday. We define their basic responsibilities. First, we are going to defend against the pass. Second, we defend against the run.

1

We will talk about coverages later as I get going. When we talk about coverages, we talk about the four pass indicators. It does not matter whether you are a linebacker, corner, or free safety, there are four pass indicators. Let's take a closer look at these points.

1. Quarterback's eyes: Where is the quarterback looking? He is going to tell you where he is going with the ball. Look for his eyes.

2. Quarterback's front shoulder: In what direction is his frontside shoulder facing? Is it up or down?

3. Long arm: When the quarterback's front hand comes off the ball, all underneath-coverage people should be breaking in that direction.

4. Ball released: Break on the ball. Everyone on the entire defense should be headed in the direction that the ball is going.

We talk about communication on pass defense. We call these *alerts.* Communication among our pass defenders is a must. There is always room for improvement in this area. The following terms are the alerts we use in communicating with each other.

1. Safeties will make sure everyone knows the coverage. Safeties tell the linebacker what the coverage is. The linebackers have a lot to do.

2. "Pass, pass, pass" should be yelled as soon as anyone recognizes that a pass is on. We want to yell as soon as we see the ball is off the line of scrimmage.

3. Yell "crack, crack, crack" on any crackback block.

4. The defensive backs, outside linebackers, and linebackers must communicate "in, in, in" or "out, out, out" when covering curls, hooks, and out routes.

5. If you suspect a tight end or slot back faking a block, yell "delay, delay, delay."

6. On a slot or wing man who is going against the grain, yell "reverse, reverse, reverse."

7. The defensive back will play pass first until he is positive that it is a run. Then he should yell "run, run, run."

8. Yell "Oskie" after all interceptions. When we intercept the ball, we want the next teammate to the ball to block the nearest receiver. Most of the time, that is the man that will make the play.

9. We must communicate with the front seven on all support calls. Every coverage must be tied in with the front seven and the secondary. They need to know, if the tight end blocks down, what type of support they have. We have to communicate with the front people to let them know what the support call is.

We start off everything with a numbering system. I am talking about inside linebacker play. Everything is built into our coverage package. We use a double-coverage call system. We will call one number that we want to play against a pro set and another number that we want to play against the twin set. The easiest way to teach it is to play one coverage versus double width. That means you have two wide receivers on one side. You have two wide receivers on the other side of the ball. It would be a pro right with a split end to the left. That is what we call a double width. Single width is when there is only one split receiver on one side. It would be twins right and the tight end on the left side. The coverage system is built so we always know that we are going to place our linebackers a certain way. We always put them to the tight-end side. The drop linebacker will always align to the tight-end side. The Mike linebacker is next. The Will linebacker will always be to the weak side. The coverages will remain the same as far as the drops. The names will change, but we try to keep it simple for our linebackers.

Let me cover the numbering system. On the pro set, the widest receiver in the formation is the number 1 strong receiver. The second receiver from the outside is the number 2 strong receiver. In the pro set, the next receiver is in the backfield, and he is number 3 strong. If it is an I set, we say it is the first back to step to that side of the field. If both backs step that way, it is the first back that gets outside. On the split-end side, there is one man split to the weak side. He is number 1 weak. If the back is offset to the split end, he would be number 2 weak.

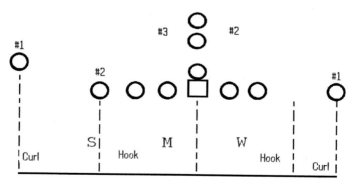

On the twin set, the widest man is number 1. The slot is number 2. Again, the back is number 3. On the back side, the tight end is number 1 weak. He is the widest receiver in the formation. If the back is offset to the split end, he would be number 2 weak.

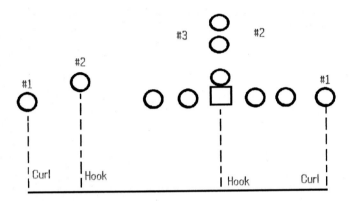

In teaching our inside linebackers, we always tell our drop linebacker to go to the tight-end side. Our Mike is strong. Our Will linebacker goes to the weak side. It does not matter whether it is pro or twins, they align to that side. We tell our Mike linebacker, who aligns over the strong-side guard, that he always covers a hook-curl area. The hook-curl area is from the nose of the quarterback to the nose of the number 2 receiver. It does not matter whether the formation is pro or twins. The hook zone is about 10 to 12 yards deep from the center to the number 2 receiver. He always covers a hook zone. His second zone is the curl zone. We tell our linebackers to open up to the hook zone. If they bring a man into the hook zone, he must cover him. If no receiver comes into the hook zone, he must widen to the curl zone.

We tell our outside linebacker that he has curl-flat zones. The curl zone is from the nose of the number 2 receiver to the nose of the number 1 receiver strong. We tell our backside linebacker that if there is no number 2 receiver on his side, the hook zone is the "ghost" tight-end area. The curl zone is from the ghost tight-end area to the nose of the number 1 receiver to the weak side. Anything outside the number 1 receiver is the flat zone. We tell our outside linebacker to open up to the curl. He works to an area 12 yards deep in the curl zone. If number 2 crosses his face, he continues on to the flat.

General Pass Defense Techniques
Zone:

1. Play run first; react to pass.

2. Execute drop technique according to coverage.

3. When pass shows, sprint to your drops while reading the number 2 receiver.

4. Drop, keeping head on a swivel, checking quarterback to receiver.

5. Wall receivers off from the inside.

Cover Number 3: Basic linebacker drops in cover number 3 will be hook to curl.

Cover 3 Progression vs. DBB, or Play Action vs. Pro or Twins

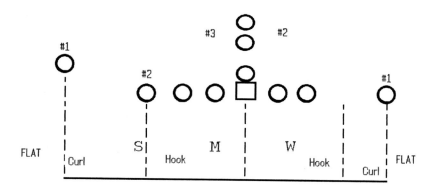

1. OG pass-sets, and ball is off the line of scrimmage.

2. Open outside to the number 2 receiver.

3. Work to the hook zone.

4. If the number 2 receiver is not in the hook zone, work to curl zone.

5. If the number 2 receiver crosses your face (drag), square up and settle, looking for the slip route out of number 1. Break up on all delay routes.

Cover 3 vs. Sprint-Out vs. Pro or Twins

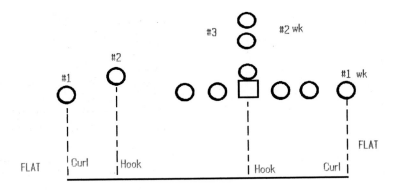

Call-Side and Backside Linebackers:

1. Sprint to: Curl

2. Sprint away: Frontside hook

Coaching point: Against sprint-draw pass, the backside linebacker must turn and sprint to the weak curl zone.

Position on receiver: When covering a receiver, keep between the receiver and the goal line. Never allow a receiver to get more than one step behind you. We will always break hard on the ball. We talk about two positions: vertical position and lateral position.

Vertical position: Not closer than 3 yards nor farther than 5 yards. The cushion will gradually come down as the receiver reaches the critical area (12 to 15 yards).

Lateral position: Keep the receiver between you and the quarterback. This is why it is important that you keep your leverage on the receiver. (We must be able to weave in our backpedal. Don't let a receiver work you head up.)

Going for Thrown Ball
1. Remember our indicators. The first thing we look for is the quarterback's eyes. The second thing we look for is the front shoulder of the quarterback. The third thing is the quarterback's hand coming off the ball. Underneath defenders break when the off arm comes off the ball. Deep receivers break when the ball leaves the hand of the quarterback. The deep defenders must do that so they do not get beat on the pump fake. If you have a

chance for the interception, shoot his hip and go for the ball with both hands. (If cushion is broken, shiver receiver.)

2. If you have no chance for the interception, make certain you tear away his backside or upfield arm and throw your other arm in front to knock the ball down.

3. If your receiver is too far away from you to tear away his upfield arm, then you must make the tackle. Be under control. The one thing I learned from Coach Lou Holtz when I coached the secondary for him at Notre Dame was this: Teams are not going to beat you throwing the football. They are going to beat you running the football. If they can run the ball, then you can't stop them. In pass coverage, it is the same way. If the receiver has caught the ball, if you can get him down and not let him run with the football, you are in a better situation. You get in trouble when he catches the ball and runs 30 more yards with it after catching it. Stop the man from running the football after he has made the catch.

4. Fight for the ball. It is your ball. I tell our defensive backs that they must be tougher than the receiver. He'd better abuse that receiver. If the receivers out-tough your defensive backs, you are in trouble.

5. Linebackers and defensive backs need to be good receivers. Look the ball right into your hands. We put them on the jugs machine. We throw them the ball in drills.

6. Hit through your receiver as he catches the ball on short and medium patterns. Make him conscious of you with good, hard hitting. You must knock the ball loose. We want to drill the receivers on short and medium catches.

7. On high passes, play through receiver's arms. We want them to play and run through the receiver. This happens on the goal line. As the ball comes and as he catches it, we want to play right through his hands.

8. On takeoff routes: When you feel that your cushion has broken, flip your hips inside, never taking your eyes off the quarterback. Work to fade on the wide receiver to the sideline. Intercept the ball at its highest point. Be ready to react to the underthrown ball.

9. If the receiver has caught the ball and is in a position to cut, you must come under control and use your open-field tackling techniques.

Chapter 2

SECONDARY DRILLS AND SKILLS

Doug Graber
Rutgers University
1993

I'm a secondary coach. I've always been a secondary coach. There is a lot of crap you have to do when you are the head coach, but I still take the cornerbacks for two 10-minute periods every day. That is my favorite 20 minutes of the day. I'm not into anything fancy. We are just talking about technique. I'll show you some of the drills we use and some of the things we teach. Some of these things have evolved down through the years for different reasons. I'm going to talk primarily about corners. I've been blessed. I've coached a lot of great defensive backs. That is the key to everything. I've been lucky every place I've been. I've had seven All-Pros and a lot of All-Americans. It wasn't because of my coaching. They were great players.

Before warm-up, we take our defensive backs on the field and work them on the sidelines on their stance and start. That is All-Pro or seventh graders. I've done it the same way all the way through. Discipline is the key. When I tell them to put their toes on the line, I want them on the line. I don't want them six inches in front of or behind the line. That sets the tone for the way you want things right off the bat. We turn our bodies in and put our inside foot back in our stance. We bend the knee and get about 80 percent of the weight on the up foot. The reason we turn in is to have a line of vision to the ball. The next thing we do is take one step back. I clap my hands, and they take one step back with the inside foot. They might gain an inch, but I don't want any more. What I am working on is eliminating the false step. With all the weight on the up foot, they have to step back.

9

Playing cornerback is not a natural thing. Kids don't grow up playing hide-and-seek running backward. Running backward is not natural. It is a taught and learned skill. The first thing they want to do is get square and on their heels. We work on keeping their weight forward and the weight over the balls of their feet. The arm movement is the same as running forward. When you start backward, you have to stay low. We start off low and have a slight rise as we go backward, but never to the point where the weight is on the heels. Vision is the key to playing in the secondary. It was enlightening to go around while I was in the NFL trying to figure out which kids had vision and which kids didn't. The hardest skill to evaluate is vision. There is no test you can give them to show it. When you are coaching the back, it is very easy to see in a week or so who has vision and who doesn't.

The next drills we would go to were carioca, hip booster, and backpedal and turn. When I went to evaluate players for the NFL, these are the drills I wanted to see players do so I could see what type of flexibility they had in the trunks of their bodies. When we do the carioca, it is not a speed thing. We are trying to get the back to get his belly button moving a complete 180 degrees every time he turns. The hip booster is a drill where the back jumps into the air and turns his hips as he goes across the field. The next drill is the backpedal and turn. I've always tried to paint a vivid picture for the kids with words in coaching. In this drill you get them into the backpedal, coaching all the techniques. The coach gives them a ball movement and they turn. But the key word in this movement is to rip the elbow to get them turned the other way. On each movement, they have to rip the elbow. Key words help the kids get the idea of what you are speaking about.

The next drill is the "W in the square" drill. The player starts off at a 45-degree angle. Once he hits the 10-yard line, he bursts in a sprint for 10 yards, then goes back into his backpedal, and then repeats the drill. That turns into the keys of getting out of the backpedal. I've heard this argued from the first days I ever coached. The key to getting out of the backpedal is being in a good backpedal position to start with. If the weight is on the heels and the body is up, you have no chance of getting out of the backpedal.

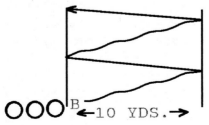

When I coached for the Chiefs, every time we played the Oakland Raiders, Al Davis would come down and stand and watch my warm-up drills. Al Davis loves corners, and we had a couple of great ones. We had Albert Lewis and Kevin Ross. He would watch our drills, and twice after games he came up and talked to me about evaluating corners. He always talked about the one-steppers. That is a guy who could take one step and be out of the backpedal. There aren't many of those guys around. I think the key to getting them out of the backpedal is not to say anything. Just put them through the drills. All body types have different way in which they operate. I don't think there is any one way to get everyone out of a backpedal. Work them in the drills and help them individually.

The kids at Kansas City helped me out with my coaching. When we played the Raiders in Oakland, the field out there was a piece of crap. It was always wet. It was awful. Our guys were slipping and falling, and it was terrible. The next year in training camp, we came up with a drill that we called our bad-footing drill. From that drill we developed our skill to get out of the backpedal. We don't plant a foot at all. We don't even mention a plant. The kids liked it, so we went to that type of thinking. We didn't teach the skill. We did drills to teach it.

The next drill is a box drill. They start off in a backpedal. At 10 yards, since they are going at a 90-degree angle, they plant their right foot and sprint for 10 yards. They get into their backpedal again for 10 yards and repeat the first movement. Then we reverse the drill so they have to plant their left foot.

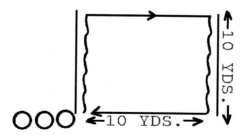

You can't do all of these drills in one day. It is a matter of repetition. We do the mirror backpedal. This is with two guys: One runs at an angle and the other backpedals. The runner changes direction on a 45-degree angle, and the defender mirrors his movement. The key in this drill is to work on your kids so they don't cross over. As soon as the defensive back crosses his feet, he is screwed. There is no way to get out of crossed feet without taking three steps. In these drills, we get them going in all different kinds of directions, because that is what happens to them on the field.

The next drill is the 3 X 10 drill, which we developed in the bad-footing drill. This is where we teach getting out of the backpedal. This is not a race, but we did time this drill to find out how quickly kids can get out the backpedal. We had a 10-yard area. We lined the backs up on one side of the 10-yard line. They would backpedal for 10 yards, then sprint back to the 10-yard line and repeat the movement. We established some norms for this drill. When Deion Sanders came out, he broke every standard I had. It broke my heart when we didn't sign him.

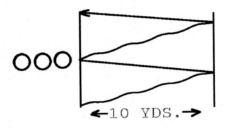

We have partner drills that we do. The first one is called "beat the stalk." You put two guys 10 yards apart. The most important thing in beating the stalk block is to attack the blocker. That helps the back for the run play where the back is throwing off a run fake. We don't run around the block. As the back gets to the blocker, we tell him to step on his toes. That is the key phase. We make contact, use the head and shoulder fake, and dip and rip through. When we get down to the dip and rip, we go outside.

Before I get into the ball drills, let me backtrack a little and tell you why we teach the backpedal the way we do. We tilt to the inside. One key reason for that is the vision. What we are looking for is what the second receiver is doing. We want to see the flow of the backs. Whether they are coming to me or going away affects what we do on the backpedal. The first priority is not having the receiver run by you and embarrass you. We take a slight outside shoulder alignment unless we have a big split. When that happens, we come in and take a slight inside alignment. If he has a minor split, we'll line up a couple of yards outside of him. As a common rule of thumb, if the backs are coming toward the defensive back, he works for an even more outside position on the receiver in his zone. If the backs are going away, the defensive backs work for more of an inside position on the receiver. We align 7 to 9 yards deep before the snap.

As we start our backpedal, it is under control. As the receiver gets closer to the defensive back, his speed picks up. When the receiver breaks the 3-yard cushion, the defensive back has to turn and run. He rips the elbow and turns his hips. We never turn to the receiver. We always turn to the quarterback. That ball is underthrown so many times. When that happens and the defensive back has turned to the receiver, he can't see the ball. The receiver can. He comes back and makes the catch, and the defensive man has to stop and make an open-field tackle. We try to convince our corners that we are going to intercept every go route thrown, and we should. As the defensive back turns, he gets width and tries to pin the receiver into the sideline. We have inside position on the ball, and we should get it. I learned that from Jack Harbaugh when he was at Michigan. It is not natural.

If you let the kids do what they want to do, they will turn to the receiver every time. In the backpedal, if the defensive back's shoulders are square, as the receiver breaks to the sideline on the go, the defensive back will naturally turn toward him. That is why we run with the shoulders tilted inside. Now, it becomes natural to tilt to the inside as he turns to run. When everything flows, you have a good technique working. A rule of thumb is to keep the back in his backpedal for 17 to 18 yards. If he has to get out of it before then, you are going to have trouble. If the receiver runs a deep comeback with the defensive back opened up inside, he has trouble coming back outside to stop the throw.

We have rules. If the backs come to us, we call that *flow.* If the back goes away, we call that *flood.* Those are Bud Carson's terms. I still use them because he is the best defensive coach I've ever worked with. With flow, we work for the outside, because 95 percent of the time the pass will be an outside route. It is just the opposite on the backs away. Because we play our corners at a depth of 8 to 9 yards, we get a lot of three-step patterns. We are keying the quarterback. When we see the three-step drop, we are out of our backpedal right now and become a man-to-man defender. When we play man-to-man coverage, the first three steps are the same as in the zone coverage. On the third steps, we get our shoulders square and play classic man to man. We key the trunk of the body and stay low. We start to mentally set down as we get into the 14- to 15-yard area and begin to anticipate routes. In man-to-man coverage, if the defenders run the go route, they turn into the receivers. The good players get their habit so set, however, that they turn inside. I allow them to do that. Teaching it to the young kids, however, I make them turn to the receiver. But they will naturally evolve to turning inside, and that is without question the best way to do it.

Let's go to the ball drills. I think ball drills are extremely important. Most kids who play in the secondary are playing there because they don't have the hands to be a wide receiver. I think it is important to do one or two ball drills a day just to set the tone. I don't know where I got this, but I've been doing it this way for 15 to 20 years. It is kind of stupid, but this is what I make them do. In every ball drill I do, I make the kids look the ball all the way down into their arms. If they don't do it, I don't make a big deal out of it. I just make them go to the end of the line and go again. I demand that the kids do the things the way I want them to be done.

The first drill is simply running straight at the coach and him throwing the ball. The defensive back catches the ball and looks it all the way down. The next one is breaking on an angle. Don't throw the ball right to him. Make him reach across his body for the ball. When I was coaching at Kansas City, that was the highlight of my career of coaching secondary. We had a great bunch of defensive backs. It was an interesting group, and when I went there, I learned some things. We had a free-agent punter from Rutgers by the name of Deron Cherry. He became a great player for us and played in the Pro Bowl nine straight years. We drafted Albert Lewis from Grambling in the third round. He didn't even know how to backpedal because all they did at Grambling was play bump and run. We got Kevin Ross in the seventh round. I went to work him out. He was 5' 8" and weighed 171 pounds. He was knock-kneed and looked funny, but he was a violent competitor. We got him in the seventh round. They were all tough, smart, and extremely competitive. Those guys averaged 30 interceptions a year for four straight years.

I began to notice that they were missing lots of opportunities on tipped balls close to the ground, so I began to work on balls low to the ground. These great athletes couldn't do it. They looked spasmodic. I got the mats out and started to work on the low ball. Pretty soon they began to catch on as to how to roll the shoulder and cradle the ball so they wouldn't get hurt. You don't want to hurt somebody doing a drill.

The "over-the-shoulder" drill is a good ball drill. We make them face inside and throw the ball over the outside shoulder so that they have to turn, locate, and catch it.

These next drills are not ball drills, but there is a ball used in them. I've been doing this drill since I was a grade-school coach, and we still do it. This is simply trying to teach kids to play zone defense and the principles of the zone. Our zone defense is really man-to-man. We are always reading the second receiver. The only time we truly do play a zone is when you have two guys on the perimeter of your zone. This is a peripheral-vision drill. This is where you are going to find out what kind of vision your defensive backs have. Line up two lines of backs 2 yards outside the hash marks. The defensive back lines up in the middle on the quarterback. The quarterback starts the receivers by taking a five-step drop. The defensive back sees both receivers and breaks on the ball as the quarterback throws. A coaching point is to coach from behind the back. You have to see what he is seeing. You have to coach his eyes. We don't break on the thrown ball. We break on the left hand coming off the ball for a right-handed quarterback. Quarterbacks, when they ball-fake, usually keep the left hand on the ball for security. We break when the left hand comes off the ball. Don't let the receiver try to catch the ball. That is a stupid way to get somebody hurt. The receivers are simply targets for the quarterback.

The next phase of the drill is to have one kid run full speed and one kid run at 75 percent speed. The defensive back has to see the difference and cheat more to the slow receiver with more depth toward the fast receiver.

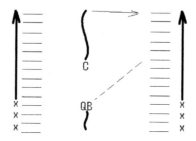

The next part of the drill is to put two guys in coverage going down the hash in the two-deep cover with three lines of receivers. Work from the middle of the field with two lines going up the sidelines and one going down the middle. The key thing in playing the two-deep zone is spacing and where they belong. If the ball is in the middle of the field and they are getting the triple streak, they belong 2 yards outside the hash marks. We start off with the toughest thing they will see. You have to challenge that kid in practice every day. I make all my coaches do it. It is important for you to explain that to your kids so the games become easy.

After that, we go to the hash marks. That changes the aiming points for the defenders. They have to play as if they are going to get a triple streak every time. The onside hash player is 2 yards inside the hash mark, and the field-side player is 4 yards outside the hash mark.

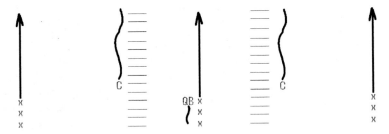

I do the corner drill every single day with the corners. We run the route and work on the timing of the routes that we think we are going to see that week. We start out with the three-step routes. We want the receiver to adjust his splits to the patterns. If he is going to run a slant, he is going to take a wider split. If he is running an out cut, he is tighter. You have to get your defensive backs to start thinking that way, too. We teach our back to turn and run with the post route. We want him running off the shoulder so he can club the catching hand. The catching hand is the one away from the throw. If the back is fooled on the flag, we teach him to wheel to get back to the receiver. We actually turn our back on the ball to get back as fast as we can. On the go route, I've talked about how we play that. However, one thing is natural. When the back turns inside, the natural thing to do is drift inside. You have to coach him to rip the elbow back and get width as he turns inside. We have to use the sideline. If you can get your kids to understand that concept, you will increase the interceptions you are getting.

The next thing that defensive back has to do is tackle. I have some drills to show you. The first one is a straight-on tackling drill with one to three moves. We don't do these full speed. We are teaching. I separate the backs into corners and safeties, 10 yards apart. I put two scrimmage shirts down 3 yards apart and make the ball carrier stay within those limits. We teach head across and shoulder into him. We are not teaching them spearing or anything like that. We want to club the arms and rip up and through. I always try to tell kids stories, because they respect hitters. If you have a great hitter on your team, everyone will respect him, and some of them will fear him a little. I always tell them stories about some of the kids I coached who were violent players. *Violent* is not a very good word, but I think it is a very vivid word when you are talking about defensive backs. Kids like that. All the great hitters that I've been around are guys that really use their arms. Watch the great hitters, people like Lawrence Taylor. Great players cock their arms. That helps them to get the timing for that six-inch explosion.

The next drill is the sideline drill. Put the ball on the hash mark, and let the tackler stalk that ball carrier into the sideline. We get to an inside position, stalk him into the sideline until he has no chance of cutting back, then really drill him.

The next thing I've added in the last couple of years. I'll tell you where it started. When I was coaching at Kansas City, Seattle set the record for turning the ball over by the defense. We had to play them twice a year. I was so impressed when we picked up a guy from Seattle on waivers. We knew he wasn't going to play a lot for us, but I wanted to pick his brain to see what Seattle was doing to force all those turnovers. I learned that from Al Davis. I shouldn't say that, but if we put a guy on waivers the week we were going to play the Raiders, Davis would pick him up just to get the game plan. I got all the drills they used, and we used the hell out of them at our place.

Here is the first drill. We do this once a week with our guys. The defensive back is put in the chase position from behind. If the ball is in the right hand of the runner, we grab with the left hand first. That is the safety valve to make sure he makes the tackle. With my right hand, I am going to make a fist, come over the top in a windmill motion, and club the ball. You would be amazed at the balls that come loose. Hopefully, you have a guy fast enough to catch someone from behind.

The next drill is a two-on-one drill. It is kind of like a Y drill. We have two defenders and one ball carrier. The ball carrier comes toward one defender; for teaching purposes, let's say he comes at the left defender. That defender would make the tackle. The second defender comes in and strips the ball. If it is in the left hand, he makes the fist and undercuts the ball. If it is in the right hand, he comes over the top. If the ball breaks to the right, it is just the opposite.

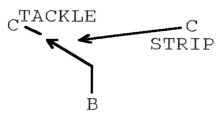

The next thing is the half-line drills, where we work our defensive back on force and tackling. On this drill, we are working with the strong safety and corner into the wide side and the free safety and corner into the boundary side. Every day you go on the practice field, you have to be prepared for what you are going to do. If you have only 10 plays with your strong safety, you want to have planned what you want to accomplish. You don't want to get out of the drill and think of something you wanted to do. Whatever offense you are facing that week are the plays you run at them. We try to split it up between pass and run.

Let me tell you how we teach the force from the strong safety. The depth of the safety is not important. It is the width that makes a difference. His rule is 4 to 5 yards outside the outside linebacker. He aligns at a 45-degree angle inside, with his feet square. He keys the triangle of the tight end, quarterback, and running back. The good ones can also see the uncovered linemen because that is the key to the force. On the Toss Sweep, he uses a knife technique. He doesn't know who is going to block him. All he knows is that somebody is coming to block him. He is coming 100 miles an hour, running through whoever is trying to block him. He is going to dip and rip through the blocker while getting penetration. He is not even assigned to make the tackle or anything else. His only rule is to make the ball get depth if it goes outside of him.

The other key is to get a fast read. If he gets a slow read and takes it on at the wrong angle, that is no good. It creates too much of a running lane. The strong safety is going to set the tone for the rest of the defense. We want leverage and position on the fullback or guard. If it means getting on the ground, that is what he does. Once you get a kid to do that, you have a player. It is not natural for a kid to do that. You must show him that he is not going to get hurt.

When the linemen pull to block the strong safety, they are not athletes. When the safety dips and rips, the lineman can't bend his knee enough to get to him. They all try to hook him or come over the top and grab him around the neck. They get all kinds of holding penalties. This is a pride point with the secondary, not only a technique.

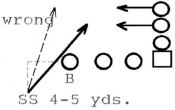

Let's talk about the rotations in the secondary. Let's talk about the three-deep zone and how we rotate for run support. We have certain concepts involved. Let's talk about a Toss Sweep as a starting point. The strong safety is primary force. The strong corner is the run/pass man. He has to backpedal until there is no possibility of a pass. He is the cautious player. After he does that, he becomes the contain man. The free safety is the secondary force man. He is an inside-out player. The weak corner is the backside-leverage player. No matter what coverage we are in, we have four guys in the secondary with those responsibilities.

I just told you how the primary force plays. If it is run flow to him but no one is coming to block him, he goes to an attack position 1 yard by 1 yard to the outside of the outside linebacker. His outside leg is back, so if the ball bounces outside, he can go get it. If the ball is totally committed to the inside with no chance of it coming back outside, he plays it from the outside in. If the primary force is making a tackle on the inside for a 3-yard gain, he is wrong. He can make a tackle for a 5-yard gain and be right. He has to be on the outside for the bounce-out play if he is unblocked.

The pass/run man is very conservative. He backpedals until there is no chance of a pass, and then he attacks the stalk block to the outside. He never comes inside any block. The only time we would ever consider that is with an extremely wide receiver.

The free safety in the three-deep keys the second receiver to the strong side. When I was coaching at Eastern Michigan, I had an outstanding safety. Everyone knew that he was a hell of a safety. On the snap of the ball, he took a little bounce step. No one taught him to do that; he just did it naturally. I got on his butt about the bounce instead of the backpedal. In a short period of time, I turned him from a great player to a very average player. I began to think that maybe that bounce step wasn't so bad. I learned a long time ago that if it is working, give it a name and take credit for it. That's what I did, and I've been teaching it ever since. I asked them to do nothing with their feet on the snap, but they can't do it. It is not natural. That is why the bounce is good. He is reading the uncovered linemen.

The backside leverage guy is the key man. Here are his rules. On a full-run flow away from him, he goes through a checklist on his steps. On his first step, he is thinking *counter.* On the second step, he is thinking *cutback.* He goes through five steps, thinking *counter, cutback, throwback,* and *reverse.* When we start out, I make those kids call out the progression. We don't yell it out in games because it

would be embarrassing. After they do that, they run at a full sprint
across the field. If they don't sprint hard in practice, they will loaf in
a game. These are habits. You have to perform the correct habits in
practice every day. The angle he takes is for 20 to 25 yards across
the field. If everybody else screws up, it is up to him to make the
tackle.

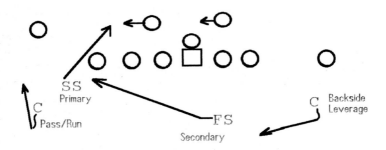

From the two-deep, the strong corner is the primary force, the strong
safety is the pass/run man, the free safety is the secondary force,
and the weak corner is the backside leverage.

On a full-run flow to the weak side from the three-deep coverage, the
outside linebacker is the primary force. However, the free safety is
considered as primary run support also, but he will get there later. He
is forcing right on the back of the outside linebacker. The weak-side
corner is the run/pass player, the strong safety is the secondary force,
and the strong corner is the backside-leverage player. We ask the
strong safety to do something that is impossible. We want him sprinting across the field at a depth of 5 yards but keeping his backside
shoulder back. That means it is a point of awareness. As he is running across, if he sees a seam start to develop, he slows down and
becomes a linebacker, moving up and filling that seam.

If there is a one-back set or split flow from a two-back set, everyone
holds until they find the ball. We don't need hard force right away
from this type of action. Once the ball flow has been determined, we
go into our same rules as before.

One coaching point in the two-deep coverage is that we don't read
uncovered linemen with the strong or free safety. On the snap of the
ball, since we are trying to disguise our coverage, our alignments
mean that we have to turn and get back quickly. In cover 2, the
strong safety is the conservative player anyway.

I'm going to give you a very simple coverage that we use. It is called "34-2-soft." We are a 3-4 defensive front, basically. We line up in a two-deep look. The 34 means that there is a three-man rush and there are four linebackers in coverage. *Soft* is a description of how we are going to play cover 2. It is a good coverage against a one-back team. If it is long yardage and you don't want to go to a nickel coverage, this is good, but if you need a strong force, this is not the coverage to be in. That is the negative of this coverage.

All four linebackers spot-drop. That means that, depending on where the ball is on the field, we are going to send them to a spot. No one has the flats. On the snap of the ball, they get to their spots as quickly as they can. They are 8 yards deep. We want them down and gambling like hell on the quarterback. We let them go on the shoulders of the quarterback. We give them a license to steal. We don't care what the receivers are doing. We go to a spot, and we are gambling on picking off the ball.

On the snap of the ball, the corners are going into a slow backpedal. They try to make it look like cover 2. The corners and safeties are reading the 2 receiver to their side. If 2 is coming down the field, they continue to get depth, playing one fourth of the field. If 2 is not getting depth, the corners settle in the flats and play cover 2. The two big negatives of this pass coverage is late force and the three-man rush.

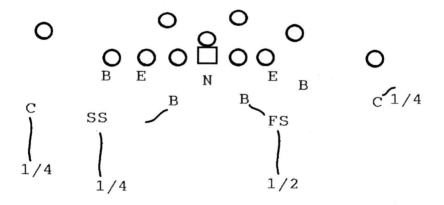

Let me give you our scramble rules really quickly. I make my secondary coach script in one scramble in our practice every day. Whoever has the backside hook is responsible for coming to get the scramble. Everyone else stays in the zone, getting depth.

Chapter 3

PRINCIPLES
OF SECONDARY PLAY

John Harbaugh
University of Cincinnati
1993

I am going to talk about basic principles of secondary play. I will cover the run-support principles and underneath zone coverage and touch on man-to-man coverage at the end. If I have time, I will talk about tackling.

If you are a secondary coach, you must realize that there is a lot of pressure riding on your shoulders. To be a secondary coach today, you need to be on the cutting edge of what football is all about because of what offensive football is doing.

Offensive coaches are attacking the width and the depth of the field. They do it with great wide receivers, great quarterbacks, and great tailbacks. I know you see it every week. We see some great players. The secondary coach is responsible for defending the width and depth of the field. There is a lot of space to defend, and it is not easy. The game of football is all about space and putting the right people in those spaces. This is where we start talking on defense. I am not going to talk about anything new.

Football is evolutionary. It all comes around and goes around. I visit with coaches who have been in the game 25 to 30 years and learn a lot from them. You can see them at the clinics. They are in the front row. They do not take a lot of notes because they have seen it all before. Last week I talked with my dad and asked him where the defensive game was headed.

When he first started coaching, the offense ran only one formation— the basic T formation. I told him that we only see that on the goal line. Dad was talking about the way the secondary would like to defend that T formation. It was a game of expansion at the time. What the offense would do would be to line up in the T formation and then expand it by running a Toss Sweep. They could run a play-action pass and expand the defense. They would force you to expand from the inside to the outside. The cornerback would line up with his outside foot back and the inside foot up.

As the game went along, things started to change. In the 1960s we started seeing another formation—the pro set with a split end and a flanker.

Now, the offense has the defense expanded. They would bring the game back down inside. How did that change the cornerbacks? The cornerbacks had their inside foot back and the outside foot up. The same was true for the strong safety. The free safety may be in a parallel stance. They would run play-action passes out of the pro set. Now, the defense has to defend seams inside.

Let's see what they are doing today. We will see this next year against Houston. They have gone to another step. They put four great athletes on the perimeter of the defense. They have two great athletes lined up on your cornerbacks. The two great athletes go against the cornerbacks. If you bring in players from the inside to the outside too far to help on the outside, they have a great athlete who will beat you inside. You can't expand too much to help on the wide receivers, because you have to defend the run. The key to defense is the secondary, if you are a defensive coach. It is an area that can get you beat really quickly.

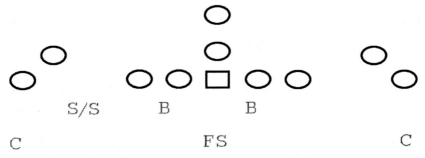

The secondary players must be fundamentally sound. They must understand spacing and positioning, and they need to be in the proper place at the right time. They need to understand the principles of playing in the secondary. Your defensive schemes need to be sound. They need to be simple, yet they need to be diverse.

The principles we are going to talk about have been around as long as football has been around. I learned them when I was young. I learned them from Jack Harbaugh, who used to coach the secondary at the University of Michigan. They have been around since football first started. The first of these basic principles happens before the ball is snapped. The players need to learn these points in meetings before they take the field.

Secondary Basic Principles

1. **Call.** A coverage call is made on every play. Adjustments or revisions may be made by the free safety after the huddle.

2. **Alignment.** Positioning is determined by call, formation, down and distance, hash mark, and field position.

3. **Stance.** The best starting body position to enable quick and aggressive reactions to start a play.

4. **Backward run.** The most-used fundamental technique executed on the snap of the ball to put the defensive back in position to play.

5. **Playing the football.** Ability to effectively know where the ball is and to anticipate and react to it when appropriate.

6. **Play recognition.** Identifying the play (run or pass) by the flow of the offense (repetitions).

7. **Execution.** The carrying out of an assignment to prevent an offensive gain.

Everything we do on defense is based on those seven principles of secondary play. That includes our drills, techniques, and schemes.

Let me go over our objectives. First is *prevent the score.* It does not matter whether you are only giving up 50 yards per game against the pass if you are giving up 500 yards rushing per game and getting 40 points scored against you. It does not matter whether no one is throwing the ball on you if the opponents are scoring 40 points. What really counts is keeping them out of the end zone.

The next thing is also important: *Minimize offensive gains.* We do not want them scoring first. We do not want them to run up and down the field on us. We do not want to give our offense bad field position. A lot of times this comes from preventing the long gain. Every Monday we look at big plays in our films. We look at the problems we have on the long gainers. We look at any run over 10 yards and any pass over 15 yards. We go over this with the players. It is our big-play film.

The third objective is to *obtain possession of the ball.* If there is any stat that is important, it is the turnover ratio. The team needs to get some turnovers for our offense to give them a chance to score.

Next come the responsibilities. These are team things, but we need to cover them.

1. Defend the opponent's passing attack.

2. Defend the opponent's end runs.

3. Defend the opponent's inside runs through convergence.

Secondary play is a game of spacing. It is a game of positioning in the secondary. It is a game of being in the right place at the right time. If your players understand where they are supposed to be relative to the ball, relative to the offensive personnel, and relative to defensive personnel, then they at least have a chance to be successful. There is a lot of room out on that field. We must teach relationships and leverage. We talk about spacing and positioning all of the time with our players.

Let me cover personal requirements for defensive backs. We talk about these all of the time.

- **Movement.** Our defensive backs must be athletic and fast. They must work into peak physical condition in order to move quickly and aggressively to the football throughout a game or practice.

- **Toughness.** (a) Physical toughness is the ability to inflict physical punishment (shed blocks, tackle, press man, roll coverage). (b) Mental toughness is the ability to endure adversity, disappointment, and success.

- **Concentration.** Concentration leads to things done correctly. Lack of concentration leads to mistakes. Physical talent must be linked with mental ability. This is the ability to do the right thing. It is the ability to be in the right place. There are a lot of things that are lumped into this: character, discipline, enthusiasm, and paying attention in meetings. They can control concentration.

Next I want to get into some individual techniques. These things go back to our principles that we covered earlier.

Stance (Normal)

1. Outside foot up and cocked slightly.

2. Feet shoulders' width or less.

3. Knees in.

4. Chest over toes, weight slightly forward.

5. Bend knees, waist, and ankles.

6. Round shoulders and arms loosely in front.

This is how we set up our drills. I am sure many of you are doing this. This is the way it looks. We put the boundary corner (BC) on the left, then the free safety (FS), then the strong safety (SS), and the field corner (FC) after that. The first team goes in the first row, second team in the second row, and third team in the third row.

Be Poised

Third group:	BC	FS	SS	FC
Second group:	BC	FS	SS	FC
First group:	BC	FS	SS	FC
Coach				

If you get them lined up like this, you will have them organized. They will know where to line up when you start teaching drills. When we have meetings, we do the same thing. We organize the meetings so we know where everyone is.

Stance (Parallel)

1. Feet parallel at shoulders' width or slightly less.

2. Weight is toward the balls of the feet, with knees in.

3. Chest over toes.

4. Round shoulders and arms loosely in front.

Be Poised: Start Backpedal

1. Push off the inside half of the front foot, while simultaneously reaching back with the back foot.

2. Maintain rounded shoulders and chest over toes.

3. Drive elbows back in normal running style to generate momentum.

4. Hips (not shoulders) move backward. Visualize being pulled by a rope attached to the waist.

There are two kinds of starts you can teach. You can teach a lead-step start and a rollover start. I do not like the rollover start. You roll off your back foot and replace it with the front foot. You gain a half step on the rollover step. We use the lead step. We use two drills to teach this. We use a visual key to start. We have the ball snapped most of the time.

Start Drill: On Line

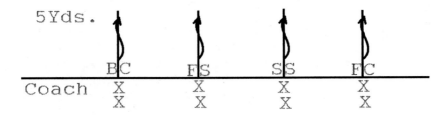

We change it up and make it competitive. We work in pairs. The first man is a wide receiver, and the second man is on defense at 5 yards. On movement of the receiver, the defense reacts. The receiver tries to touch the defender before he can get back 5 yards. The receiver is running forward, and the defender is running backward.

Start Drill: Touch Defensive Back

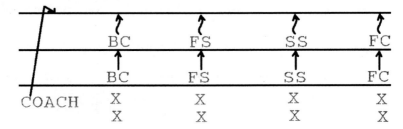

Sprint

Backward run should be fast and under control. Think quickly!

1. Pull yourself over the balls of your feet, as opposed to pushing off the front foot.

2. Maintain body position.

3. Reach back just beyond the hip.

4. Keep feet close to the ground. (Imagine your cleats brushing tops of blades of grass.)

5. Pump arms in a strong but relaxed manner.

We want them to be fast, but we want them to be under control. There is a way to measure the backward run. If a player runs a 40-yard dash in 4.8 seconds, he should be able to run a 30-yard backpedal in 4.8. You can time them in both to see whether they are getting back fast enough.

Backpedal: On Line

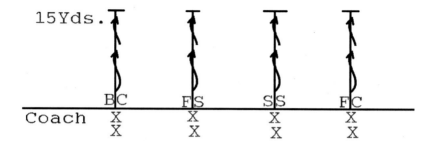

Backpedal: Competitive

Break and Drive

This develops the ability to transfer backward movement to forward movement. We change from the backpedal to the forward run. We never stop our momentum. We *redirect* it.

1. Drive instep of the foot that is opposite direction of break into the ground.

2. Quickly place second step down and toward interception point.

3. Drive second-step knee to the ground, roll over it, and accelerate to point.

Keys: Think quickly! Maintain center! Accelerate off break!

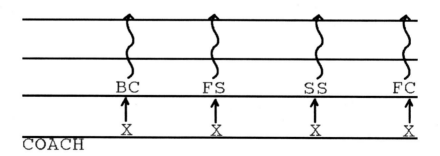

Break-and-Drive Drill

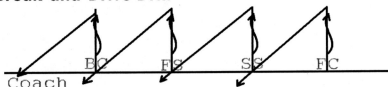

Open and Run

This develops the ability to transfer movement from the backward run to the forward sprint as the receiver closes the cushion.

1. Maintain a cushion as long as necessary (15 to18 yards). Danger point is 3 to 6 yards from receiver on stem.
2. Your body follows your feet. Toe-in the opposite foot and jump-turn side foot to open hips. (Foot used is relative to man or zone coverage.) Head will bring body in man. Widen to squeeze-fade in zone.

We use visual keys on the drill. We use the ball boy to throw the ball to one of the two men on his side. The coach throws one ball to the two men on his side. By using the ball boy, we can get more action for the defensive backs.

Open and Run: Hip Turn

Turn on line; one step; stay low; play ball; work drill both ways.

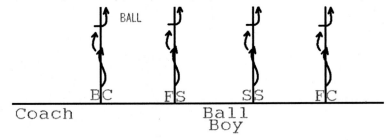

Open and Run: Deep Fade

First step; fade; play ball.

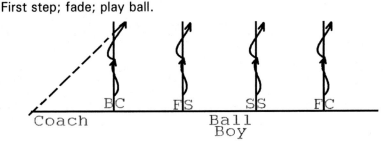

Open and Run: Post
Work deep balls every day with wide receivers if possible.

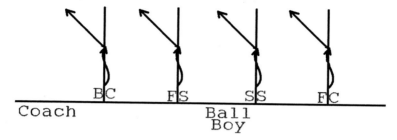

Playing the Ball
This develops the ability to go get a thrown ball and make transition to an offensive player. Incorporate a ball into every applicable drill. This is an ability that can be developed through practice.

I want to include our secondary run-support responsibilities. This will give you an idea what we are talking about as we go into more details.

Secondary Run-Support Responsibilities
1. Primary force. To constrict and contain the play. First defensive back in run rotation.

2. Secondary force. To defend the play-action pass. To tackle the play-side breakthrough.

3. Cutback. To defend play action. To prevent a long gain on the cutback run.

4. Backside contain. To defend play action (throwback, reverse, etc.). To prevent a touchdown run.

Drills
1. Pursuit

2. Run-Pattern Recognition

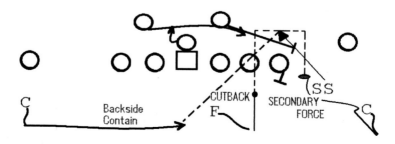

We want to define everything we do. We do not leave anything to chance. All four secondary players have a responsibility on the run. Here on a strong outside run, the strong safety has the primary force. He is responsible for turning the ball back inside. The second man in the rotation is the second man on the strong side. Here it is the strong corner. He has secondary force. He is a pass-first player. He is responsible for the deep outside one third. He is a secondary force on the run. The secondary force will be 4 to 6 yards behind the primary force man. We do not want two primary-force men. We ask the secondary force to be the backup for the primary force.

The backside has responsibility. The free safety is the third man in the rotation. He has the cutback. He is 1 to 2 yards inside the primary force and 4 to 6 yards deep. We have built a triangle for the defense to stop the run. If the ball bounces outside, we move outside and keep the ball on our inside shoulder. It is spacing; it is a game of positioning. The backside corner has the backside contain. His job is to prevent the touchdown. Here we apply the 21-player rule. He is responsible for keeping 21 players in front of him.

Defensive Backs' Run Techniques
Knife: Used by strong safety versus strong outside; run in three-deep coverage.

Stance: Parallel
Alignment: Normal (3-5 X 4 on TE)
Key: Backfield through Y

Technique Progression
A. Outside-run-to-key rule: If blocked, attack blocker. If unblocked, settle on line of scrimmage; pitch.

B. Sprint through knife course to target (1 yard outside, deep back).

C. Variations versus run pattern: Recognition.

1. "B" (tripod or pry technique): Constrict with outside arm and shoulder free (hand sweep).

Dagger: Through FB (I Toss) Drills
1. Run-pattern recognition

2. Dagger versus bag

3. One-on-one reps versus defensive back (punch drill)

4. Live versus FBs-OGs

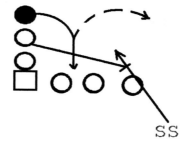

2. "G": Take collision point to lead lineman. Pry: Hit on rise! Whip and replace: Shorten G's course.

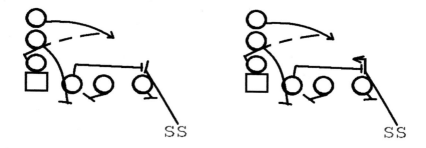

3. Arc: Attack Y on knife course. Tripod/rip: Collide and shed to pitch. Whip and replace: Maintain leverage on pitch. Fan iso: Leverage to ball.

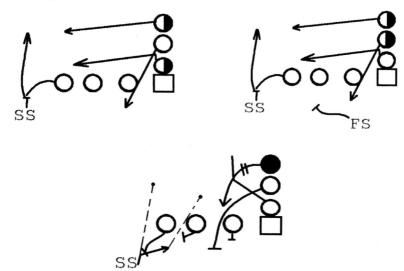

4. Crack: Note split; tighten alignment; beat it! If can't beat it, tripod or whip and replace.

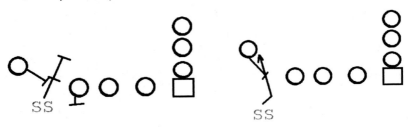

I want to talk about man-to-man techniques. You can teach an okay athlete to be a good man-cover player if he understands position relative to the man he is covering. If he is fast, he can be great. Our base man coverage is inside man.

A. Inside Man (Base man-coverage technique)

    Stance: Normal

    Alignment: 6 to 9 yards, inside attitude

    Key: Quarterback to receiver

Technique Progression

1. Key quarterback with peripheral awareness of man. (Drop key quarterback to get good break on quick routes.)

2. Backward run (shoulders square), maintaining inside leverage (weave).

3. Break and drive on all cuts from inside cushion position.

4. Recognition point and interception point.

5. Versus vertical routes

    = Man turn: Hook hips; play ball relative to position achieved.

    = Hook hip: Play ball to quarterback.

    = Chase: Play ball to man.

B. Press Man (Man-cover technique executed from line-of-scrimmage alignment. May screw or bang from this alignment.)

    Stance: Parallel

    Alignment: Line of scrimmage, inside attitude (variable)

    Key: Man

Technique Progression

1. Take away quick inside route by base alignment (change-ups).

2. On snap, baby-step back and out.

3. Time opposite arm jam to pressure the release.

4. Stay on top of receiver and generate vertical momentum.

5. Run to get hook-hip position. Flip if man gets to your tail side.
   Key: Feet; jam; run
   May "worm" to defend C.W.M. fade/post.

C. Inside/Outside (I and O)

Connie call used by corners when 5-yards rule in effect. When playing both-corners loose man. (May press split end and avoid Connie call.)

Technique Progression

1. BC is generally inside; normal inside technique on inside receiver. Take number 1 only when number 2 runs flat/switch route.

2. SC is generally outside; outside zone technique. Take number 2 only versus number 2 flat/switch route.

D. COMBO (Man-cover technique used to double-team a receiver and add secondary support to run defense in man coverage)

Stance: Corner—normal; FS—parallel

Alignment: Corner—cover 3; FS—cover 3

Key: Corner—quarterback to wide receiver; FS—wide receiver

Technique Progression

1. Corner: Play press technique at 6 yards. Play run such as roll. Primary force. React to route of number 1 versus pass:

   Number 1 across—Rotate deep one half—number 2 vertical

   Number 1 vertical—Outside man

   Number 1 outside—Outside man

2. Free Safety: Gain inside cushion position on number 1; play inside man technique; secondary force versus run.

I want to make a point about tackling. All of this material is good, and there are many things you can do in the secondary. You can use all kind of disguises; you can use man coverage or zone coverage. All of this does not mean a thing if the secondary can't tackle. This has been a problem for us at UC. Guys get into position to make the play but do not make the tackle. Whatever you do, teach the guys how to tackle. The first thing you should do when you walk on the field is to teach the tackling drills. That is the most important thing.

Chapter 4

DEFENSIVE MAN-TO-MAN TECHNIQUES

Tom Holmoe
University of California
1998

As a defensive backfield coach, I am going to give my players the weapons and tools they need to be successful. They need to choose them very carefully. I'm going to start with presnap reads. Some of you may not be defensive back coaches, but I know you can learn from these things. Everybody is a creature of habit. Everything we do we do repetitively because we are comfortable with the way we do it.

The first thing a cornerback has to know is Down and Distance. The next thing is Field Position. We want to know what they like to do when they are backed up, in the middle of the field, and when they are in the red zone. The best professional organizations have tendencies about things they do. The third thing is Formation. This is where you start to get some things that really count. Here is an example: We were getting ready to play the Green Bay Packers in 1995. They didn't run slot formation very much. Every once in a while they would run it. Any time the slot receiver was off the ball they would run what people call "Smash," or a quick look-in. If the slot was on the ball they would run a sprint option. The split end cleared. The slot went to the flat. The back cut the rush end and Brett Favre would sprint out and throw the ball. That is all they did from that set. That was the Green Bay Packers the year they won the Super Bowl. The sad thing is we knew that going into the game and they completed three out of five passes.

The fourth thing a corner should see is the Offensive Line. The corner wants to look at the offense and see whether it is "Heavy or Light."

When it is going to be a run, the offensive line is heavy in their stance. They have their weight forward, ready to come off the ball. On a passing play, they will be light with their weight back. When we play Tennessee, they run 50 percent of the time and throw 50 percent of the time. If we can determine whether they are going to run or pass, we have cut down the plays by 50 percent that we have to know. If the defensive back goes through his checklist of tendencies, by the time the ball is snapped he has eliminated about 85 percent of the plays they run. That is a good advantage for the defensive backs.

A fifth big tendency is Time on the Clock. The defensive back has to be aware of how much time is left on the clock. If it is early in a game there are certain things they will do. If it is late in a game there are only a certain amount of things they will do. When time becomes pressure, some coaches will panic. When the two-minute period comes around, the number of plays an offense will run has dwindled. There will only be about five plays that an offense will run in the last two minutes. If you know the five plays, that is a tremendous advantage.

Now, let's go to the wide receiver checklist. As a corner you have to be cool. You have to have a lot of composure and poise. We are talking man coverage now. I want my corners to watch the wide receiver coming to the ball. The first thing to check is to see if they are looking at the sticks. If they are, they are thinking first down. Does it matter how far they have to go to get to have a first down, if he is going to be blocking for a run? He wants to know how far he has to run in a route to get a first down. I'm not saying this will happen every time, but if that is how it comes up, it is something to think about.

The second thing a corner looks for is the wide receiver counting off to himself the distance he wants to run the pattern. If the receiver is looking up the field and trying to find an aiming point, that is a pass, not run. If it is a run and they have a crack block to execute, they don't even look at the corner. They are trying to find their blocking assignment. If it is a pass and they are going to run the route off the corner, they don't look at the safety. Where the wide receiver is looking is a key to the play.

That is why I want the defensive backs out of the huddle fast. That gives them time to observe all these things. I like to be there so that as the defensive back takes his alignment on the receiver, he has time to false move on the receiver. That means after the receiver sets, move the defensive back inside. If the wide receiver readjusts to the alignment of the defensive back, it probably means he has a blocking assignment on the corner and is getting closer. If the run is coming his way and you are 3 yards inside of him, he has a bad angle. It is a game to see if you can get him to adjust. He won't readjust if he is running a pattern. If, after the defensive back moves, the receiver stays put, the defensive back simply realigns knowing it is probably a pass play.

The next key is the width the receiver is from the sideline or offensive set. The pro hash marks and numbers on the field are at different places than the college hash marks and numbers. One of the things the Dallas Cowboys do through film study is to find out at what distance a team will not run an out. When a receiver aligns in that position, they play him hard inside anticipating a curl, slant, or some kind of inside move. With an offensive set we like to look at the distance between the split-side receiver and the offensive tackle to that side. If his split is relatively tight he is probably trying to make room to the outside to run a pattern or get closer to his blocking assignment.

Look to see the distance the wide receiver is off the ball. Getting up in a press situation on the receiver will tell you a lot of things. If it is a run, the Z receiver wants to crowd the line of scrimmage as much as he can and still be off the line. He wants to get up there so he can get a piece of you. If it is a pass, that same receiver will back up a little so he can get that extra separation to get away. When that happens we get off the receiver and start to think pass. Sometimes, when you get off, the receiver will sneak up a little. This confirms the fact that it is a pass.

The next one is one of the fun ones. I give little prizes to the defensive backs who find mannerisms in wide receivers while watching films. Make a game out of it. It is fun to get your guys to look at film. I give away a candy bar or some type of award if they can identify one of these mannerisms in a wide receiver. I remind myself of this by the Babe Ruth story. Everyone remembers him as a great hitter and forgets that he was also a pitcher in his early career. He was getting hammered in this one game. It seemed that everyone was sitting on his fastball. What they found out was, that as he threw the fastball he stuck out his tongue.

Watch the mannerisms of the wide receiver. If he comes to the line of scrimmage drying off his hands, more than likely it is a pass. If he is going to block he doesn't care whether his hands are dry. It is a nervous habit. He probably doesn't know he is doing it. We had a receiver in the pros who would adjust his sweat bands every time it was a pass. I know you are thinking that is no big deal to know whether it is run or pass. As a defensive back that puts you that much farther ahead and it will help you.

The reason I'm talking about this is that I know that most of the guys in this room don't have corners who can really run. You might have one corner who is pretty good but I doubt there is anyone in this room who has two corners who can really run and cover. You are holding your breath for most of the game with your one corner. The reason I know these things is because I was one of those slow guys. I had to know all these things I've been telling you about or guys would be running by me all day.

The next thing is the quarterback checklist. There are some really good ones in here. This one gets a lot of defensive backs in trouble. The first one is speed to the line of scrimmage. One of the things that screws up the corner in his coverage is the quick count. He is not ready. He is kind of getting into his set and going through his mannerisms and the ball is snapped. He is not ready to backpedal.

What I want is for the defensive backs to go through their looks at the receiver and then look in at the quarterback. Most of the time they have time to do that because the quarterbacks generally take their time looking over the defense. They are trying to get the presnap read, also. If you see the quarterback delay coming to the line and everyone else is still, it is going to be a quick count. If those linemen are down and set and the quarterback is kind of hanging back, that means quick count. Linemen usually take their time getting down and adjusted. The quick count usually comes on a pass play. It helps if he can relay that across the defense. The linebackers should really see that.

When I played with the 49ers, I was a second-team safety. I played behind Ronnie Lott. In practice I played against Joe Montana. He did the same thing every time. He looked right, then left, called his cadence, and snapped the ball. After the snap his eyes were right down the middle of the field. You couldn't get anything off him. The other guys would look to where they were going to throw. They would check it out. A lot of times they would never look to the other side. If I'm a defensive back, particularly a safety, I want to know where the quarterback is looking. Some quarterbacks will look the defense off, but most of them don't have that ice in their veins to do that. Tell your defensive backs to find out where the quarterback is looking before the snap of the ball.

Watch the quarterback when he breaks the huddle to see if he licks his hands. They might even do it in the huddle, but most of them do it at the line. They want the feel of the ball. A lot of them won't do that on a running play.

This is a big point. This kills a lot of people at the college and pro levels. This is the automatic. I listened to the Washington State offensive coordinator yesterday. He said when they read the pressed man-to-man, they automatic to the fade. I tell my defensive backs when they hear the automatic, they change their position. If they are in a pressed man they get off. If they are off, they get into the pressed position. If the corner is back and the quarterback automatics, what is he going to call? It doesn't take a genius to know. He is going to the slant, hitch, or quick out. A lot of teams don't call a play in the huddle. They step in the huddle and call "Check With Me." The play is called from the line of scrimmage.

It is essential for a corner in coverage to know who is helping him and where they are. Communication on defense is the number 1 problem. If you are playing with a safety in the middle of the field, playing free, the corner's technique is different than if he has no help. We play a lot of quarter cover. My corners and safety work out games on the field. Before the snap, if my corner knows he has help inside and reads a tight split by the split end, he tells the safety he is going to jump the out. He knows the safety is over the top. If the corner reads the wide split, he tells the safety to sit on the curl and he will get over the top. I want them to do that. On the other side they can't do that. If the tight end runs the seam, the safety has to pick him up and can't help the corner. They have to know that and communicate it to one another.

The next thing is shifts and adjustments. These are things that happen before the snap of the ball. If the receiver is off the ball you should think motion. The defensive back has to think, if he goes in motion what is my adjustment? He has to do that before the ball is snapped. Have the corner tell himself in his mind what he is going to do.

It is very important for the safety and corner to that side to echo the call made in the huddle. We have a rule that they physically look at each other on every single play. That is in case the safety sees something and wants to make a change, the corner won't be so locked in on the receiver that he misses the defensive change. When I got to pro ball from college, it was amazing to me how much talking was going on during a defensive presnap. When you break the huddle in pro ball there is constant chatter. In high school there is dead silence.

There is nothing being said. They have to talk and tell each other what they see. They have to tell each other how they are going to adjust.

Finally, we get into nonverbal signals. This gets kind of crazy. You may not use these much. Sometimes you can't hear. We have all these nonverbal signals for things that happen late. It keeps you from blowing the coverage. We can see it in the film. How many times has a kid said, "I never heard the call change"? Well, there it is on film. We can see it. We spend a lot of time on presnap reads. We do it at all positions.

What I'm going to get into now is what I call "The Three-Step Drop." This is one of the tools you give your corner to help out to a big degree. I am firmly convinced you cannot teach your corners to play just press or bump-and-run. They have to be able to play off. You have to have a variety of things to throw at the receivers. There are some guys in the NFL who are great press guys. They dominated their guys in high school and college because they were faster, bigger, and stronger. They got up on them and mauled them at the line. When they got to the next level they didn't have the skills to play off the receiver. You see some great first-round draft choices that don't know how to play off. You need to teach your guys that. It is easier for the nonathletic corner to play off.

We play 9-10 yards off the line. The outside foot is up and the inside foot is back. I believe you have to have your hips and shoulders square in man-to-man coverage. That is a fundamental for football. If the ball is inside, I can keep my feet square, see the receiver, and see inside with a slight head turn. If my inside foot is up, I can still see by turning my head, but I can't see the safety as well. What we are looking at is the three-step drop. We are trying to cheat and get more knowledge before the play is run. We are looking and anticipating a three-step drop. What drives me crazy is to have a corner 7-8 yards off the ball and on the snap he starts backpedaling. They throw the hitch, slant, or an out. The ball is caught and the corner has the same cushion as he did when the ball was snapped. That is ridiculous. It is unnecessary even for a guy that is slow.

The defensive back has gone through his presnap read of the receiver and quarterback. His head goes back to the quarterback. I want him to throw the three-step drop. We don't want the defensive back to take anything for granted or assume anything. The quarterback takes his first step. His second step is shorter and he gathers himself on the third to throw. If it is a three-step drop the defensive back knows the pass routes. They can only run hitch, slant, quick out, screen, or fade. We have eliminated a lot of the patterns that receiver can run.

I learned this in 1983 when George Seifert was the defensive coordinator and Ray Rhodes was the defensive backs coach. They had picked this up from the Philadelphia Eagles. They had some corners who weren't fast. They played them at 10 yards. On the snap of the ball they did not move. As soon as they recognized the three-step drop, their eyes came back to the receiver. They looked to see what the pattern was and drove on the route. They didn't backpedal or bail out and they are going to close the cushion. The fastest guy that they have and the slowest guy that you have created no problem on this play. This gives your guy a chance to make the play.

We study the drops of the opponent's quarterback. They take the first long step, a small second step, and set up to throw. After studying this we can tell the three-step drop on the second step. We don't have to wait for the third step. In the five-step drop, if our corners see the fourth and fifth step in the drop they have gone too far with the quarterback. After the defensive back sees the second step, he knows it is going to five steps. If the quarterback takes one big step and a second big step, it is not going to be a three-step drop and the quarterback is going to five or seven steps. Now, he looks at the receiver and starts to work on the route. It takes a while to drill this, but it is the way to play. The key is the eyes. Once they read the drop, their eyes go back to the receiver and never come off him until they make a play on the ball. The number 1 screw-up in man-to-man coverage is the eyes.

If the quarterback rolls out or play-action passes, that is a five-step drop. If he rolls or turns his back to you, forget about the three-step drop. The routes on rollouts are going to be outside routes. The one that is hard is the sprint quick throw. He sprints but is looking to throw on the third step. You have to live with that.

The presnap reads are the defensive back's tool. It is going to eliminate the things that they can do and gives the defensive back a greater sense of what they are going to do. The second tool is your ability to read what is going to happen in the play before it happens. Recognizing the difference between three- and five-step drops eliminates even more what they are going to do.

The stance in the man coverage at 9-10 yards off is simple. I'm not going to spend much time with it. If they are in their stance, I don't mess with it much. I leave that up to the individual because he is 10 yards off. Don't force them down into an uncomfortable stance. Let them play a little high. As long as they have the outside foot up and inside foot back, and are on the balls of their feet, I let them play. I also want good balance in their stance with hips and shoulders square.

Any time you see the head going up and down as the defensive backs backpedal and break on the ball, that is bad. That is the first thing we can see. We want smooth movements with the head on the same plane all the time.

One of the cardinal rules in man coverage is once the eyes go to the receiver, never look back to the quarterback. The mistake that all defensive backs make is when the receiver makes his break, they want to look back to the quarterback. That is bad. Focus your eyes on the receiver at all times. This is a common mistake by defensive backs. The receiver starts upfield on the go route. The defensive back is on the inside of the receiver and turns to run with the receiver. The quarterback is inside the defensive back. The defensive back's eyes go upfield where he is running. The receiver breaks off a comeback move and the defensive back doesn't see it because he is looking upfield instead of at the receiver. The defensive back's eyes have to be where he is at, not where he is going.

As the receiver runs at the defensive back, he doesn't want to look into the receiver's eyes or at his head. He concentrates on his jersey number. As the defensive back turns to run with a receiver, that is when we start to concentrate on the eyes of the receiver. That is learning to play the ball.

One of the things you are going to find, which is a problem with defensive backs, is "Tempo of Backpedal." I use a drill where I backpedal them slow and then I increase the speed to fast. The defensive backs have to be able to backpedal and change their pace. We backpedal at the same rate as the receiver is coming off the ball. If he is coming off fast and you are backpedaling slow, he eats up the cushion. If he comes off easy and you backpedal fast, you increase the cushion. Receivers come out hard and slow down so they can lower their hips and break. I teach our backs they have to adjust and mirror the tempo of the receiver in their backpedal.

I teach this drill where they start out slow, then speed it up. Then they go back to slow and then back to fast. What you see when they go from slow to fast, is their heads being thrown back and their bodies coming up. Remember, we want the head on the same plane at all times. If they can control the backpedal, they can adjust to the receiver's run.

Never give a receiver a two-way go from your alignment. If the defensive back aligns on the midline of the receiver, he is beat already before the ball is snapped. That is the worst thing you can do. Take something away with your alignment. In a split position we want to take away the inside. If the receiver is aligned real tight we may want to take away the outside. If you take away the outside you better be asking for help before the snap. It is a lot tougher to throw the out than it is to throw the curl or an inside route. When we align on the inside, my defensive backs are thinking they have taken away the inside by alignment, now break on the out. If it is a good throw and catch they might complete it. If they throw the inside route and I keep my leverage, I am in great position to take the ball away.

If the receivers start to stem their patterns, the defensive backs do the same thing. I use a drill to teach this.

I start them in the middle of the field and backpedal them all the way to the sideline, gaining depth as they go. What they have to do is backpedal and step and slide.

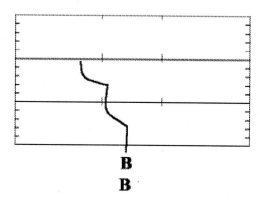

When a receiver starts his pattern, generally he comes off hard. He stems to the inside, and what does the defensive back do? The big mistake he makes is to turn his shoulders inside. That is what the receiver is looking for. When he sees that, he breaks his pattern outside. They want to break the cushion and turn the shoulders of the defensive back.

The question always comes up about what is a good cushion. You can't answer that because it differs from players you have and every opponent you face. Don't go into a defensive backs' meeting and tell them the cushion we are going to run is 5 yards. If you have a 4.5 guy and a 4.8 guy, it doesn't work. Cushion is something that is always changing. With the read technique I use, fast corners can play it at 7-8 yards. Deion Sanders would line up 6-7 yards and just stand there. The receiver would close the cushion to about 3 yards to the point you think he is beat. Deion would just turn and catch them in nothing flat. Some guys can't do that.

Let's talk about the turn a defensive back makes as he turns to go deep with the receiver. The key to the turn to run deep is the shoulder. If you can get them to dip the shoulder as they turn, it keeps the head level and keeps them down. When guys get beat on go routes most of the time it is the speed. But the rest of the time it is the turn. They have great backpedal, but when they go to turn they get high. The receiver is running forward and the defender is running backward and they lose him in the break. We work on that every single day. It is not a dip that pulls your head down. It is a momentum dip to turn the body.

Another problem with turning is the way to turn. Do you turn into the receiver or away from the receiver? In man coverage you turn into the receiver. In zone coverage always turn to the quarterback. In man coverage the defender turns into the receiver and has his back to the quarterback. The defensive back has to see the receiver and focus on him all the time. As I run deep with the receiver I want to turn my back to him as I go for the ball. A lot of coaches say to turn into the receiver. I'll tell you why I don't coach that. As I turn with the receiver, if I am within one arm's length of him, I am in position to look back for the ball. If I'm not within one arm's length of the receiver, why would I look back for the ball? There is no reason. Don't look back; run to the receiver and make the tackle.

If I am within one arm's length, I turn into the receiver and aggressively go for the ball. If I turn my back to the receiver I may see the ball for a longer period of time. If I turn the other way I see it only as it comes into the hands of the receiver. As the defensive back looks back for the ball, he wants to look up. He doesn't look back for the ball. That's where the quarterback is. If he does, the ball might come over the top and drop into the receiver. He has to look up to find the ball. This rule is for the open field. It does not apply in the red zone. In the red zone the defensive back cannot turn his back to the receiver because the ball is going to be thrown high and outside. He will never see it. You have to drill that hard.

If we are locked in a go pattern and we are only 10 yards downfield, don't think the ball is coming out that quick. There are three signs when to look. The first one is the eyes go up. The second is the hands come up. The third is the arms come up. You have to focus on the eyes first. As the defensive back turns for the ball he drops his hand onto the hip of the receiver. That keeps him from losing contact with the receiver. If the receiver starts to adjust out to the throw, I don't see him but I feel him and go with him. If the defensive back gets his hand up into the chest, that is pass interference and I think they will call it. Down low on the hip I don't think it will get called. If the defensive back's head is back looking for the ball, the referee will let you get away with a lot of stuff.

On the break the defensive back wants to mirror the break of the receiver. When the receiver runs by a defensive back on a go route, the defensive back has to make a complete turn so that he is running straight down the field. The mistake is not to turn all the way so that the angle of the run is toward the sideline instead of down the field. I do a drill with backs that shows this problem. Backpedal your defensive backs down a line, have them turn and run deep. Our good defensive backs turn and stay on the line. Our freshmen have trouble staying on the line. They bubble out and off the line because they do not turn their hips all the way. They take three steps when they should have taken one. If you are 4.9 like me, you better take one, not three steps. That simple drill will give them confidence they can do that fundamental thing.

This is like advanced football. Good defensive backs have a sense of when the ball is coming on a deep route. It is hard to say this about high school quarterbacks because they are so inconsistent. But college and pro quarterbacks we can make this statement about. If you were to take a cut up of every deep route thrown in the NFL in a given year, I would say that 85 percent to 90 percent of those balls will be caught between 42-45 yards from the line of scrimmage. If a quarterback takes a five-step drop and throws deep, that ball will come down in that area. Some quarterbacks have big-time arms, so why doesn't the ball come down 48-50 yards downfield? The answer is simple. The receiver can't get that deep.

Here is a coaching point for defensive backs. When they go for the ball, punch it with the fist or slap it with the hand to the ground. Don't knock the ball up in the air. Get it to the ground if you can't intercept it.

Chapter 5

DEFENSIVE PERIMETER TECHNIQUES

Bobby Johnson
Furman University
1996

We take pride in playing physically tough football. This means we are going to attack the line of scrimmage, swarm to the ball, and strive to be great tacklers. We also stress to our players the importance of being *Mentally Tough*. We want our players to play as a team, execute when the pressure is on, and to play with confidence.

We want to execute when the pressure is on. This is a player thing and a coaching thing. You may be able to play great in practice, but you must be able to perform in the game. That means, as a coach, you must put the player in a position in practice that he will see in the game. A lot of planning goes into setting up the practice schedule. The players must learn to execute under pressure.

We are going to try to play with confidence. This was the key to our improvement on defense this year. We gave our players a lot less to do, and hopefully that made them more confident in what they were doing.

We are going to try to be fundamentally sound. That is probably one of those Dick Tracy comments. Everyone wants to be fundamentally sound. We are going to stress several things. This is what we do to stress the fundamentals. In our teaching methods we have always stressed two important principles: *Learn What To Do*. In other words, know where to line up, know the adjustments for any shifts, motions, or unexpected formations, and know your responsibilities while reacting to the offense. When a player can't get lined up, it upsets me more than anything. We try to get them lined up in the right spots

49

at the right time. The players must learn to make adjustments. They must learn to react. They must *Learn How To Do It*, which means they must use the proper technique in each situation.

In 1995 we were extremely inexperienced along our defensive perimeter. We started out against Georgia Tech with very little experience. In our secondary, our strong safety had 45 plays of experience. The free safety had 13 plays of experience. One corner had 37 plays the year before, and the other corner had never played in a college game. All of our backups in the secondary had no game experience at all. At linebacker, we started a freshman and two sophomores. Because of this inexperience, we felt we had to be extremely simple on defense. We think it paid off. We ended up second in the conference in pass defense efficiency, second in touchdown passes allowed, first in third-down conversion prevention, and did not allow a pass play over 37 yards, which occurred in that first game. Georgia Tech beat us 51-7, but did not throw the ball very much, or the score would have been 100-7. But we got a lot better after that game.

We looked at our defense and decided in the spring to keep it very basic. We ended up limiting ourselves to basically one front and one coverage with two variations. We played that basic defense 80 to 90 percent of the time most of the year. If you have seen us play, or if you have heard me lecture at a clinic, you know we always line up in a Weak Shade front with a rotating or prerotated 3-Deep Coverage.

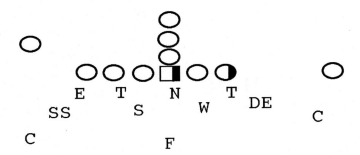

As other teams started to spread us out with one-back or no-back sets and forced us through elaborate adjustments by shifts and/or motions, we thought it was important to simplify and give ourselves the ability to adjust easily. We feel that we accomplished this by going to a 4-3 look by turning our drop end into an outside linebacker.

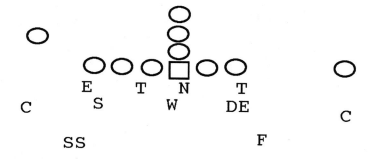

We declare our front to the tight-end side or to the one-receiver side when there is no tight end. We feel that we have a gap control system with our front seven versus the run. We change up the secondary support with our two coverages.

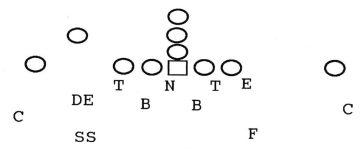

In our Cover 2 Read, we will get run support from our corners. If there are two receivers to one side, both the corner and the safety are reading the number 2 receiver at the snap. The key question is this: Is the safety being threatened? If number 2 is blocking, the corner will commit to the run and be the contain man on that side of the ball. At the same time the safety must look up the number 1 receiver to deny any passes off the line of scrimmage or play action.

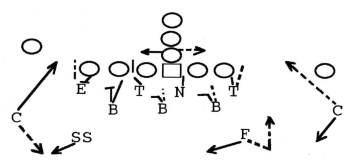

If number 2 does not block the corner we must read the release of number 2 to determine his technique. In our Cover 2 Float, we get run support from our safeties. The safeties read the ball at the snap of the ball to determine if the ball is *On* or *Off* the line of scrimmage. If the ball is on the line of scrimmage, the safety will find number 2 and he will support if number 2 is blocking. The corner must stay over the top of number 1 to prevent play-action passes. If there is no number 2 receiver the safety will support as soon as he sees the ball on the line of scrimmage.

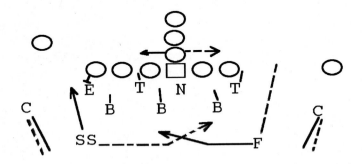

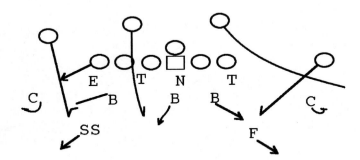

Against the pass in Cover 2 Read, the corner and the safety are still reading number 2. If number 2 releases to the flat or goes across under the linebackers the corner will squat in the flat and the safety will play over the top, preventing the post, and fly from number 1 in that order.

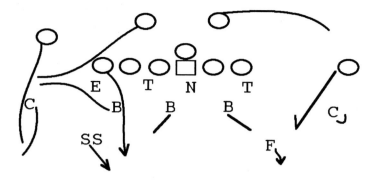

If number 2 releases vertically, the safety must cover number 2 and the corner must stay over the top of number 1. The outside linebacker on the two-receiver side must know what release number 2 is giving. If number 2 is going to the flat, the linebacker knows that the corner will squat in the flat and take that area. The linebacker must go to the curl and deny the ball from number 1. If number 2 releases vertically the linebacker must be prepared to pick up number 3 in the flat because the corner has vacated the area because of the release of number 2. The middle linebacker must not let number 3 go vertical and he must be prepared to open up to the side if number 3 releases and then hunt up number 1 or number 2 if they are coming inside.

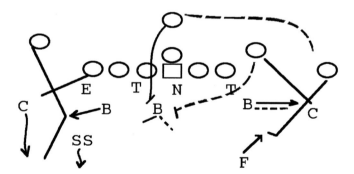

Versus the pass in Cover 2 Float, the corners will always stay over the top and play their one fourths. We may cheat the safeties up a little. We are now going to support with the safety. The safety will read the release of number 2. If number 2 goes flat either way, the safety will hunt up number 1 and look to rob the curl. The safety is aggressive and tries to read the route stem to determine whether the receiver is running a curl or a post. The linebacker to that side will work through the curl to the flat. The middle linebacker opens to the side number 3 releases to and looks for receivers from the outside.

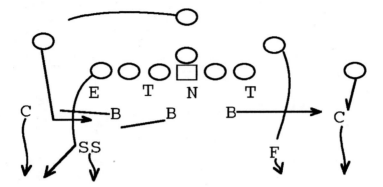

If number 2 releases vertically, the safety must insure him while the outside linebacker still works through the curl to the flat.

We feel this coverage is a good complement to our 2 Read coverage, especially when offenses start to run adjustment routes and put pressure on our corners and safeties with the flag routes.

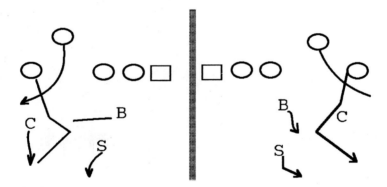

The corner and the safety end up with a good bracket on the flag, and the linebacker is working to the flat or the under route.

Basically we played our 2-Deep Coverage with the corners outside at about 6 yards. The safeties were lined up at about 12 yards. Our basic rule for the safeties was this: They are going to split the difference between the wide receiver and the tackle. They are never going to be wider than the offensive side hash, or wider than 2 yards outside our hash mark. We are going to give them a landmark so they can line up properly.

Chapter 6

PRESSURE SECONDARY COVERAGES

Jim Lambright
University of Washington
1996

Let me go through a couple of things about that weird position called defensive backs. Everybody has picked them apart with the Shotgun Formation, One Back, Multiple wide receivers, and things like that. The most demoralizing thing in the world is to give up the big bomb right away. We don't go out and try to coach caution to our defense. With 11 guys up around the line of scrimmage, we certainly don't look like we are cautious. We want to make sure we are taking away the offense's biggest plays. Whenever you go in with a game plan, find the offense's best receiver. Find the best route and design a way to stop it. Make them beat you with routes they haven't shown they're good enough to beat other people with. The first thing we want to do is take their strengths and make them beat you with something that has proven to be their weakness. That goes for the run or the pass.

To stop the big play there are a number of things you have to do:

1. Make sure you contain the ball. That is to keep the quarterback from scrambling as well as having good force on sweeps.

2. Eliminate mental errors. We want them to have a balanced offense and defense. We want enough to win but not so much that the players are confused. If you have a player who doesn't understand, then you, as the coach, haven't done a good enough job of teaching. He is either in the early stages of understanding where you have to walk him along, or he has to be taken all the way back and start over again. Maybe you've asked him to do too much. Be careful with the mental part and how much you are

challenging them. Make sure you don't overload them. You may be a genius, but if they don't reflect that, you need to change something you are doing.

3. No foolish penalties.

4. Missed tackles are one of the things that lead to big plays.

5. Think turnovers.

6. Make good judgments.

7. Do the little things.

8. Play with your pads over your toes.

9. When to look for a pass. Look for a pass after a time-out, following a delay-of-game penalty, the first and last play of a quarter, or after a substitution. Look for the pass in these situations.

I think it is critical that your team think positively. Think interceptions and turnovers. That is the concept of, "Is the glass half full or half empty?" If there is one thing I want to teach and believe in, it's that we are going to be 12-0 next year. I am the flaming optimist. If I think we are going to be 11-1 next year, I'm already defeated. Which team am I giving a win to? Your team has to think prior to the snap. We want them fully in the game. A lot of this starts in the huddle. Do you have a guy in the huddle who reminds everyone what the down and distance is on offense and defense? How many of your linemen don't have the slightest idea how the downs are progressing? We make sure we have someone in the offensive and defensive huddle who is keeping them up on what the situation is.

We have flash cards for our defense. They are situation cards with Screen, Draw, and Pass written on them. We have a coach on the sideline who holds them up. We have a player on the field who is responsible for looking for them. My corner coach is great. He is so into the game. He is a great young coach. But he stands on the sidelines and yells, "Screen, Draw," and goes through his checklist. It is amazing how few players are paying any attention to him. He does it a lot out of nervousness. We use the card to get a clue into the game, so we don't have to scream and yell from the sideline when nobody has been assigned to listen to you.

We have a statement which is always in our notebook that defines what your secondary has to do to stop the end run and run-pass. It is necessary to have three elements.

1. You need a primary force man, who also has the pitch on the option.

2. You need a cutback man, who is responsible for the quarterback on the option.

3. You need a secondary force man, who takes up the support if primary support is lost.

We are always going to have someone playing over the top to make sure there is someone there for the play-action pass.

The primary force man has to play the run from the outside in. If he can make the tackle, he makes it from the outside. His key is generally the end man on the line of scrimmage. As soon as we can, we want to tie them into reading the linemen because it is so much faster in the read. We want them to be focused. We give them something to look at all the time.

The cutback is an area of varying width. Hopefully, it is as narrow as possible. It is the area between the outside pursuit man and the first inside pursuing lineman. He is the first man running inside-out to the ball. He is the man making the play right after the primary force has turned the play in. He is also the man responsible for the quarterback on the option. His cutback responsibility can be increased or made impossible by a force man who leaves too much of a cutback gap. The angle of force becomes critical to the cutback player. The secondary run support are the people that pick up the support if the primary support gets blocked.

On the force angle, you want the narrowest lane possible as a cutback lane. We want our force man to play games with his depth. We want the force to think pass first. He takes his shuffle or read step first. If he reads absolute run blocking, he comes up with the aiming point on a tight formation as the outside hip of the tight end. I would rather teach a young player to force too tightly and let the play bounce outside him than make him too cautious to begin with. If you start off with a too careful concept, you have a more difficult time getting them to be aggressive, if you correct the aggressiveness and make him a little more cautious. We want the shuffle step and a hard tight angle to make sure you get as much penetration as possible to the lead blocker, making sure he keeps leverage on the ball carrier. If the rover gets cut, the corner is the secondary force. The free safety comes on the fill for the cutback. The last line of defense is the man in the deep third away from the play. He is the touchdown saver. He is the last man in our pursuit angles.

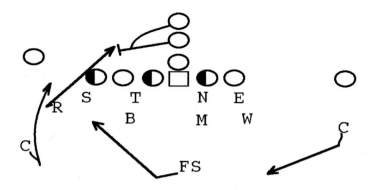

If we are facing an option with the Sky Coverage, we play it differently, depending on whether there is a lead blocker. If there is a lead
blocker, we play that as if it were a blocker on a sweep. The rover
goes and gets him. If there is no lead blocker, the rover sets on the
line of scrimmage and feathers the quarterback. He stays with the
pitch man, but he doesn't open up a big cutback lane for the quarterback. The force angle changes with a lead blocker or no lead
blocker. If the quarterback cuts up with the ball, the rover still has
the pitch and stays inside out on the pitch. The quarterback is not
his responsibility.

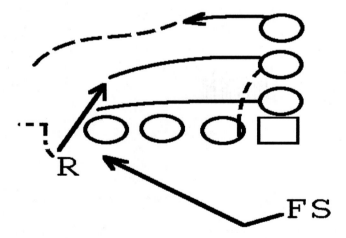

The thought behind Cloud Force is a team that cracks the force a lot
or a short split by the wide receiver. We always give our guys a rule
on the split based on the game and who we are playing. I don't
particularly want my corner forcing. Now it is a matter of how the

offense gets him to become a force guy. The same rule pertains to the corner as to the rover. If he has a lead back, he attacks it as deep and tight in the backfield as he can. He plays the pitch on the line of scrimmage like the rover. As we look at this set, the whip or weak-side end has fill on the quarterback, with the free safety coming over the top for the secondary force away from a wide slot. This is a single-width formation, with no wide receiver to the whip side.

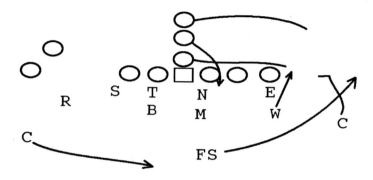

The Easy Force is a linebacker force. To the split-end side, we can let the whip force. He has the same rules as the rover on the lead blocker or no lead blocker. To the split-end side, the aiming point is 1 yard outside the last man on the line of scrimmage, to the depth of the lead blocker, assuming the ball carrier is inside the blocker. He attacks that as tight as he can. The corner has secondary force, and the free safety has the cutback. Easy Force against the option with no lead blocker, the whip stays on the line of scrimmage and plays the pitch. He feathers the quarterback but has responsibility for the pitch man. The free safety has the quarterback coming inside out.

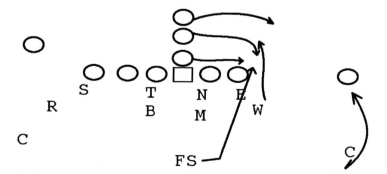

We use our free safety a lot in the running game. We have not been hurt over the top, even though he was a much better run player than he was a pass player.

Toward the wide slot our primary force comes with the Sky Force or the rover. His aiming point is 1 yard outside the offensive tackle. It is only the aggressive point. It is the point where there is no cutback. We try to cheat the rover so he is in position to fly after he takes his shuffle step. Our rover or strong safety is an aggressive person. He may be overly aggressive. He is a linebacker almost, put out in coverage. The best ones here don't want to shuffle step. They want to fly. They are people who like to cause great collisions in the backfield. They would prefer to do it out-of-control and kamikaze-style.

The worst thing you can do to a player who naturally has a good instinct for contact is to give him too many rules. If you want to screw up a guy from making big plays, start to give him things to do. The more you give him to do, the more he will slow down. When you have a really good one, turn him loose. Let him go blow things up. Let him make some mistakes, but have somebody coming from inside out or outside in to kind of cover up for him. The best thing in the world is to have a player like that and get him somewhere around the line of scrimmage. He will destroy the outside part of people's running game. He also comes great on passing situations. As long as you let him do what comes naturally, it is amazing how much you can get out of an instinctive player like that. It is playing within your system, but recognizing his talent. We have put him on the line of scrimmage and brought him on dogs and crashes and not made him responsible for contain. We tell him to go under or over the blocker based on your decision. Let him make the choice, but cover up behind him, to take care of whatever bubble that is not bleeding.

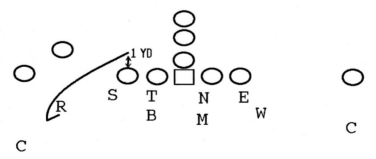

We get an awful lot of crack against our Sky Force. If you get some tendencies of teams that like to crack, it is important for the corner to call the crack to your rover. If the slot is trying to crack on the linebacker, the rover has to yell crack to the backer. When I was coaching linebackers, I told them the first time they got hit in the head by one of those really physical wide receivers, he had permission to go out and hit the corner the way the receiver hit him. It was amazing how fast corners started calling crack. I would rather have the player be wrong than not say anything. Don't worry if you're right, just talk. We want our kids to talk while they are doing their agilities. I don't care what they talk about. They can talk about their dates, for all I care. What we want is their mouth and feet working at the same time. It is amazing how hard it is to get them to talk if you don't ask for it. At every position we do this. There is so much communication that has to go on that it is really important to practice talking. When we are going through our warm-up drills, you hear every position talking. This is a good time for us to emphasize the talking part of football. On the crack, the corner calls the crack and becomes the secondary force.

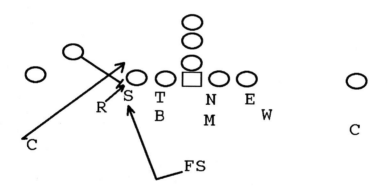

Let me talk to you in specifics about our key defense and then I'll go to coverage responsibility. What I really want to do is talk about how to design your secondary. I'll go through Cover 1 and 4, which is a 3-Deep and Man Free.

I'm not trying to sell you on our Cover 1. The front is called "G." Our front is an eight-man concept, which can become a seven-man concept. That is based on what we are guessing you are going to do. It can also be a nine-man concept, based on the front look and disguise. What do you need to be sound and to win? For us, playing Cover 1 has been a real good defense for us. It gives us the ability to be a nine-man front. We have eight men up already with the four-man down front and rover, backer, Mike, and whip as linebackers. We can play all sorts of adjustments with these players. We use the free safety as a sweeper. If we are playing an option team, the free safety knows he has dive, to quarterback, to pitch, going both directions. If the dive breaks we want him to break down and make the tackle. It the running back doesn't have the ball, he keeps going on the quarterback and helps out on the pitch. He truly is a middle-of-the-field player. In his coverage he is reading the release of the number-2 strong receiver.

The rover and whip are underneath curl-to-flat players. They also have any wheel pattern coming their way. The wheel route is any flat player turning his pattern up deep. We ask them to play over the top of the wheel pattern. They drop out under the curl routes until an inside receiver crosses their face to draw him out of the curl area. We had a field and boundary corner last year, because we had only two corners in the program that could play.

Our field corner was faster than our boundary corner. If we were in the middle of the field, you could see the quarterbacks looking for the slow corner. You knew you had to do some things to help him.

The corners are playing an Inverted Half. They are responsible for playing over the top of the number-1 receiver and playing half coverage deep like a Cover 2. The thing I like about this is I have my physical players playing run, and the coverage players playing pass. If you want to get into a 2-deep philosophy, you will end up with two safeties back deep. The corners are truly coverage people, and all the other nine can play run. We do not have a nickel package. We do not substitute. It could be third and 57 to go on the last play of the game, and you will see the same people out there for us.

We play with the people we have. We disguise like we are coming and end up in zones or man coverages. When you substitute nickel and dime people it may look like you are smart. It doesn't mean you are putting a real smart player on the field. You are putting a player out there who hasn't gotten nearly the repetitions your starters have. If they have a quarterback, he will look immediately for the new guy. Here is a guy who is not good enough to be in the starting 11. They find him and go at him. The conclusion we came to was to leave the guys on the field who were getting all the practice time.

The backer and Mike linebackers are responsible for what we call Back-to-Curl. If the back releases out of the backfield and comes vertically downfield, they play him man-to-man. If the back does anything besides coming down vertically, the linebackers take the curl to their side. They become curl replacement players. If the back comes out to the flat, the rover or whip takes the flat, and the backer and Mike linebacker become the curl replacements.

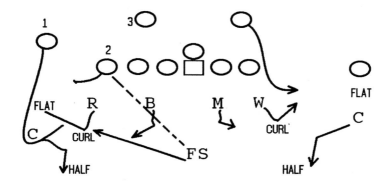

The free safety is reading the number-2 strong receiver. He is taking number 2 on all vertical routes almost man-to-man. If number 2 runs an outside route, the free safety comes over and robs the curl area to the strong side. He becomes a middle robber unless number 2 comes downfield. It ends up being a man and zone deal with two half players over the top. I'm not trying to sell it to you. I'm just trying to show you what's been good for us.

Here is a Cover 4, as we call it. It is a 3-Deep Coverage with the free safety in the middle third and the corners in the outside third. The rover and whip have the same coverage underneath, except they are not responsible for the wheel, because they have a third player behind them. This is a safe cover. But you give up something in run support.

The Mike and backer linebacker are playing hook-to-curl zones. We backpedal our Mike and backer out. I want them thinking draw and screen first as they start to drop. I don't want them turning and thinking they have to run. It is our goal to be a great run defense first. That will get you farther than being a great passing defense. When they are sure it is pass, they open their hips in the direction the quarterback is looking. If the quarterback turns to the strong side, both the Mike and backer's hips open strong. The rover is already the curl-to-flat player. The backer squeezes the hook-to-curl zone, and the Mike linebacker watches the backer's back.

They keep their spacing as they open. The whip drops under the curl and will never go to the flat as long as the quarterback is looking away. He works back inside. That gives us an advantage because the linebacker can cheat and squeeze the zones.

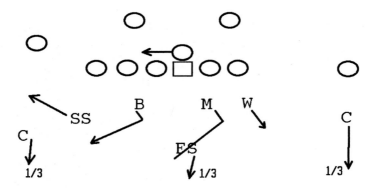

All the adjustments that are made in coverage are done by the under-neath people. Let's look at a Pro Set with the halfback set to the split end. The set gives a running strength to the tight-end side as far as numbers go on the line of scrimmage. But there is a backfield strength that is much more important to us in terms of the linebackers. The offense will have trouble running a play to the tight end from this set. It takes too much time to get there outside of the guard area. We *bump* our linebackers. The whip comes to the line. The backer aligns across from the lead back or halfback. The Mike linebacker cheats to a strong A gap. We want to make it hard for the offense to block the 3 shade and Mike linebacker in combination. We bring the rover into a bump position in a stack behind the stud end. It is like the linebackers are tied on a string. When one gets bumped over, the other moves also.

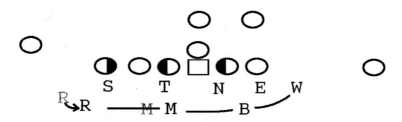

If I draw it up against the strong back set, the bump goes the other way. Rover steps out toward the line. The backer linebacker is at least on the strong back but maybe a little wider. Mike moves over, and the whip comes back to his position over the backside tackle. With the back in the strong set it is hard for them to run anything outside the guard to the weak side.

It takes a long time to get that back outside going weak. Getting people bumped over takes away a lot of the angle advantages people try to get with motion or shifts.

Cover 4 is a great coverage for a balanced attack plan. When the offense goes to a 3-receiver side, it is not so good. We would check out of Cover 4 against a trip set and go to Cover 1. We don't need many people to the back side. They have a single-width formation with no wide receiver to the tight-end side. What we do is play the corner over the top of the outside receiver to the half. The free safety still has the number-2 receiver strong. That leaves two zone players underneath. The rover has the curl-to-flat and maybe a wheel. The backer has the hook-to-curl. The backside corner is almost a free player. We want him to cheat as much as the offense allows us to. If they block the tight end, the corner plays all the way over the top into the middle third. We tell him to use his vision. As long as there is no one coming in his area that is a threat deep, he helps out to the strong side. He moves into the middle looking for routes coming to the post. It is really hard for the quarterback to pick up that weak corner playing over the top.

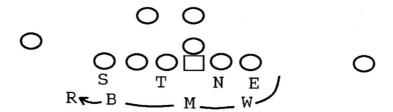

The formation that gives us trouble because of the stretch is the four-wide receiver look or two tight ends and two wide receivers. That gives you a real stretch up the middle of the football field. The zones don't change, but the free safety has to really be careful on the tilt of the quarterback's shoulders. We hope the rush is good enough not to let the quarterback look one way and have time to come back the other way.

Another set is the Empty Set. That is, no backs in the backfield. In that situation, we would prefer to pressure that formation. If we have our choice when the offense empties out, we check to pressure. The worst thing in the world is to see the quarterback drop back with a three-man rush coming. They have you blocked, and they have five guys out on a pattern. Your secondary is scrambling their butts off to cover. The thing that we want to do is make sure we get somebody to him. We can come with an inside or outside blitz. It doesn't matter if there is no running threat other than the quarterback. I'm one of those guys who hears someone complain about the injuries to quarterbacks. My first thought is, "Why don't you keep somebody in to block for him?" They spread people all around the world and then complain when somebody comes free and kills the quarterback.

We would play a zone and bring pressure. We want to always bring one more defender than the offense can block. The reason we went to pressure in the first place wasn't because of the tight power formation. It was because Arizona State came into our stadium and had between 700 and 800 yards of total offense. We were at home and couldn't even slow them down. It was a one-back set. Their quarterback may as well have had a thousand yards in the game. We couldn't even start to compete with them. We can't let teams spread us all over the field and not have a way to get somebody to the quarterback. When I had a chance to visit with Buddy Ryan, and saw his 46 defense, it was pretty much the same way. Buddy's philosophy was to bring one more than they could block until it was back to two tight ends and three backs. That's the way football is supposed to be played.

This is a quick look at our man free from our basic four-man front. We play a free safety with our corners locked on the wide receivers. Then we count strong and weak. The rover takes 2 to the strong side. The backer takes 3 to the strong side. The Mike and whip work in combination on number 2 to the weak side. If he goes outside, the whip takes him. If he comes inside, Mike takes him. If we want to, we let Mike have him and rush the whip. This allows you to bring 5

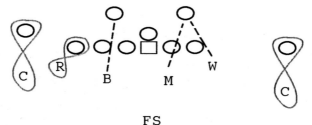

and have 6 in coverage with a free safety.

With this thinking you can bring your free safety on a dog. He can blitz any number of gaps. With good timing the free safety can give you a tremendous rush up the middle. We want him on the snap of

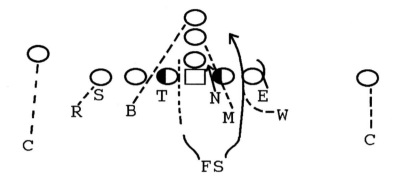

the ball to be about a linebacker's depth. If he can disguise it well, it can totally screw up all the blocking for the linemen.

If a team goes to a wide slot and tight end, we could cover 1 and 2

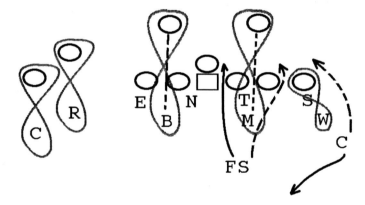

weak with the Mike and whip and have the corner free. That gives you all kinds of possible rushes or coverages with two free readers.

You could blitz the free safety and still have the corner in free coverage or bring the corner in a rush scheme.

In our 46 look we play a 3-deep zone or man free behind it. We started out putting our rover on the tight end since he was our best coverage man. When we did that, he got killed on the run. The linemen were drawing straws to see who got which body part. To stop that we moved the backer over to cover the tight end. The rover now has 3 strong or takes any back either way who becomes displaced from the set. He is the adjustment man. The corners have the 1 receivers. Mike and whip combo number 2 weak, or run a stunt with

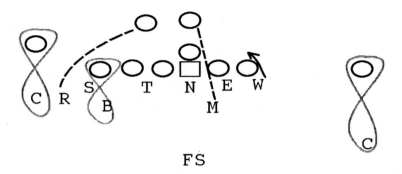

FS

one of them coming. The free safety can align about 5 yards deep if he wants. He can cause a lot of problems because he is the unaccountable player.

We never want rover and whip on the same side of the formation. They are the curl-to-flat players. We can put the corners on the same side in twins or trips and not have any problems. If they go to the wrong side of the formation, it's okay. But they can't be wrong on the same side of the formation. That is when we have problems. The Mike and backer are hook-to-curl players always. They don't have any curl-to-flat responsibility. As you look at all these adjustments, it is a lot easier to pressure people and make them keep people in to block. The good thing about the 46 look is it does put pressure on the offenses. It forces the offense to go away from something they wanted to do that they thought was simple. It makes the offense think in terms of simplifying the offense to work out the blocking schemes.

When you prepare for game day, look at how much time you are spending adjusting your offense or defense to adapt to what your opponent is doing. Take out the things that are too complicated. That is when we took out our reduction defense. We are spending all our time adjusting it to a balanced look because of the spread offenses. What we did was to spend all our time adjusting to them instead of finding ways to create problems for them. You don't want your opponents controlling your whole practice and particularly the games. Spend time developing things that will force that offense to adjust to you. Do things that take them out of the things they want to do. Take your best players, give them some tools, and take away whatever your opponent does best. That gives you the best chance.

Chapter 7

TWO-DEEP SECONDARY COVERAGE

Art Markos
University of Virginia
1995

We are a 4-3 Front with a primary Two-Deep Coverage. That is not the only coverage we teach, but that is our primary coverage. I'm going to talk about our drills as well as our scheme.

In teaching pass defense at Virginia we break it up into three groupings. The first group is the run package. When we talk about outside runs, options, and play action, the secondary is responsible for support and fill. Flow passes make up the second grouping of our pass defense. Flow passes for us are when two backs start in the same direction and the ball is leaving the line of scrimmage. We have a prescribed coverage for flow passes. Even though we called two-deep coverage we go to a different mode. The third grouping is where the ball is in the pocket with no fakes. What I am going to talk about is when the ball leaves the line of scrimmage, the backs have split. We have three different modes of our teaching in pass defense.

In 1991 we ended the season with 12 interceptions. In 1992 we had 17 interceptions but we gave up a lot of long pass completions. When I say long, I mean the gain was over 20 yards. We analyzed that season to find out what caused those long gains. Every time there was a long pass, the primary underneath defender had gotten too much width and not enough depth. Something made that defender get too wide in his zone to be able to make a play on the ball. With that in mind, we went into spring practice in 1993 with the thought that depth was more important than width. In 1991-92 the percent for passes completed over 20 yards was 16 percent. In 1993-94 that figure dropped to 10 percent in 1993 and 11 percent in

1994. The interceptions went from 12 and 17 to 22 and 27 in those respective years. That was in regular-season games only. They don't count bowl games and two-point plays in those stats. On a two-year basis we increased our interception rate about one interception per game.

In our zone package we have two-, three-, and four-deep zones. We also teach a quarter–quarter–half, which is a combination of two- and four-deep zones. We also have man coverage.

When Rick Lantz came to Virginia, in the development of the secondary, he wanted a list of requirements by positions. The players knew the bare minimum required by his coach to do his job. I came up with these requirements for the defensive back positions. I also used these to grade my players:

1) Stance and Start

2) Alignment and Assignment

3) Key Read

4) Leverage on the Ball and/or Threats

5) Tackling

6) Aggressive Movement to the Ball

7) Corners—Physical Jams; Safeties—Hard Read on Quarterback's shoulders.

None of these requirements has anything to do with physical ability. It has to do with an understanding of your position and performing the basic requirements of the position.

To begin our teaching for the two-deep coverage we defined our zones. From the line of scrimmage to 6 yards down the field we define as the "No Cover Zone." There is no one responsible to be in that zone to cover someone. From 6-20 yards going from the outside in, we have the "Flat." The next zone is the "Curl." That is defined as 2 yards inside the normal alignment of the number 1 wide receiver. The inside of the Curl and the outside of the next zone, called "Hook," are 2 yards outside the normal spacing of the tight end. The "Hook" zone goes across to the point of 2 yards outside the normal alignment of the other tight end. The other two underneath zones are the Mirror Curl and Flat on the other side. The Flat goes to 20 yards deep for us. The "Halves" are broken up by the middle of the formation.

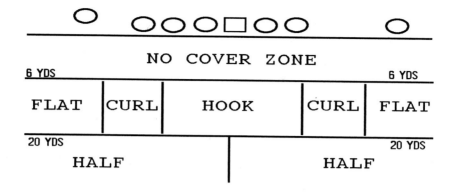

We define the normal formation spacing. In the middle of the field, if the wide receivers are aligned 9 yards from the sideline, that is normal. Anything wider than that would be an abnormal split. If the ball is on the hash mark the field receiver is normal if his split is not wider than 5 yards outside the other hash mark. The boundary corner has a rule of no closer than 6 yards from the sideline. A wide receiver into the boundary would be on the numbers to be normal.

Here are some things that I have emphasized as a secondary coach. On the field and in meetings these are the things that I emphasize and drill:

1) Vision—see the entire picture on your side of the formation (including linemen).

2) Disruption—of routes whenever possible.

3) Location—within your zone. Depth is more important than width.

4) Reacting—to the ball thrown. Short defenders—take chances; deep defenders—take fewer chances. In practice we want all our players to see what their range is. They learn that in practice, not in games.

Next, let's talk about our alignment in the two-deep coverage. The alignment for the corners is 2 yards outside the normal-spaced receiver and 7 yards deep. The strong safety to the two-receiver side splits the difference between the normally spaced tight end and wide receiver and 10-12 yards deep. The free safety has a two-man leeway from the ball to offensive tackle. That is a lane so he can see the ball and put himself in a position to cover his half. He has a decision based on the split of the wide receiver to his side as to where he aligns.

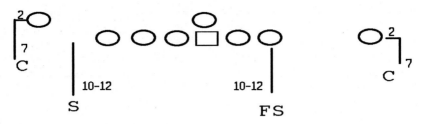

The stance of the corner is cocked-in with his inside foot back. His hips are actually facing a point about 3-4 yards inside of number 1. There are two reasons for that alignment. If they are the primary support on a running play, that is the angle I want them to start on. They may not get to that point but that is the angle. I want their eyes going through the end man on the line of scrimmage on their side and into the backfield where their keys will be. Their knees are bent and their feet are shoulder width. The safeties bend their knees with the feet inside shoulder width. I want them to bend at the waist so that the shoulder pads are over the knees. I want their inside foot back in a reactive kind of position.

We teach keys and responsibilities. The secondary keys the release of the number 2 receiver to their side. The strong corner and safety are working independently of the free safety and quick corner. We consider two-deep coverage to be a balanced cover; therefore, the four defensive backs are working independent of each other.

I'm going to tell you about the Linebacker drops. The starting angle of the Sam Linebacker is a point 2 yards outside a normally spaced tight end 12 yards deep. He may not get there but that is his aiming point. The Mike Linebacker starts on an angle for a point 2 yards inside a normally spaced tight end and 12 yards deep. The Will Linebacker's aiming point is 2 yards inside a normally spaced tight end and 12 yards deep.

The first pattern I usually work on is 4 streaks. The safety controls the inside vertical area of the defense and the corner controls the outside vertical area. We do not take any read steps by the corner or safety. Once we read pass we move in the direction we need to move. The safeties back up straight and the corners hold. The corner is 2 yards outside the wide receiver. He holds his position so the wide receiver has to exaggerate his move if he wants to get outside the corner. He holds his position as long as he can.

Once the receiver gets within 2-4 yards, the corner has to move for position. He moves inside the number 1 receiver, keeping his eyes on the number 2 receiver. Once the number 2 receiver passes the 5-yard mark, the possibility of the read route is diminishing. At 5 yards, because of the tight end's speed tempo, the corner can read whether he will continue deep or break his route off. If the corner makes the determination that the tight end is going deep, he positions on the inside of the number 1 receiver and carries him deep.

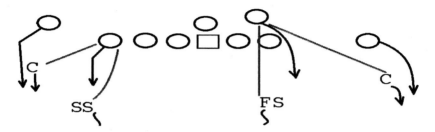

The corner cannot get an effective jam on receivers positioned to their outside. Receivers in front of or to the inside of the corner can be jammed. We like the jams to take place at 10-12 yards. Jams that take place at a deeper place in the pattern affect the timing of that pattern. The wider the receiver goes, the deeper the jam. We get to a point on the receiver's inside. We don't want to get in a hurry on our leverage side. When I first started coaching this, I told our backs to deny the receiver the outside and knock him out of bounds. The corner wanting to please me got too aggressive in trying to knock the receiver out of bounds. The receiver found it easy to head fake, get inside the corner, and zip down the field uncontested. That was a problem because the safety has read number 2 up the field on a vertical route.

The safety is going to be closer to number 2 than number 1. He is not exactly splitting the difference between the two receivers. He favors the tight end coming vertical. We don't want the corner to get in a hurry going to the outside to play number 1. If he can jam number 1, fine. If he can't jam him, that is all right, too. The thing he can't do is let the wide receiver inside him down the field.

As the receiver breaks from the line, the corner's hips are in position to run. He has his vision on number 2. If number 2 breaks out, the corner settles and gets his vision back on the quarterback. He wants to be ready to break deep on the fade or inside on the read route. He wants to leverage the read route from the outside in. The linebacker is leveraging the number 2 receiver from the inside out. If the safety sees number 2 break to the outside, his only threat deep is number 1.

He weaves off his original angle and moves toward number 1. He doesn't turn his hips.

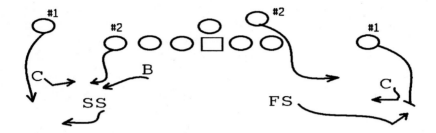

The third thing that can happen is number 2 runs vertical and runs the corner route. The number 1 receiver hitches up at 5 yards and the number 2 runs a corner route behind it. The corner can read almost from the beginning that something is going on. We tell the corner to hold his depth until he is threatened from the inside out by depth. If number 2 is 4 yards off the line of scrimmage and the corner is aligned at 7 yards deep, he isn't being threatened from the inside. He doesn't feel any pressure until the tight end gets even with him.

The corner reads the slow pattern by the wide receiver and sees the tight end still going vertical. The corner begins to position himself. His hips are to the inside and he works for a point back 12-14 yards deep. The corner is responsible for the throw on the corner route up to 20 yards. The hitch by the wide receiver is in the no-cover zone. If they throw the ball there, we react up and make the tackle. The safety comes off with the corner route and takes anything beyond the 20-yard mark. A technique we use is called "hard read off the

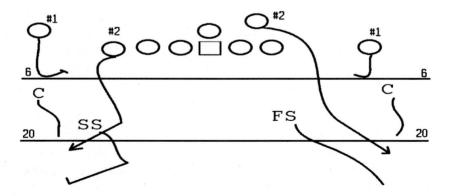

quarterback's shoulders." When the quarterback gets his feet set and has his shoulder cocked in a direction, we want the linebackers and 4 defensive backs to cock their shoulders in the direction he intends to throw. We don't want to square up any time. We feel the reaction left and right is less from that position.

The next part of the progression is with number 2 going across. The corner generally gets inside stems out of the wide receiver. With the tight end going across, there is no other threat to the flat except the wide receiver. Number 3 coming out of the backfield is not a part of this coverage. The corner slides in with depth and width and gets extremely aggressive with the wide receiver. The corner jams and funnels the wide receiver in toward the safety. He runs deep and on the outside of the wide receiver. There is nothing else that can threaten the flat. If the number 3 receiver comes to the flat, the Sam Linebacker takes him there. When the safety sees the tight end go across, he takes the inside post away from the number 1 receiver. He is also responsible for the dig route. The free safety takes the dig route like the strong safety. He carries his coverage across the formation if the quarterback is on the run. It becomes a man coverage for the safeties on the post and dig routes.

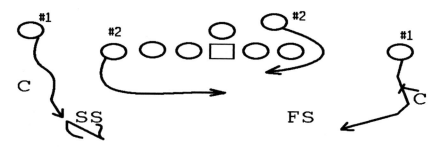

The last thing that can happen is for the number 2 receiver to release to the flat. If the receivers are normally spaced, the corner starts to move in and positions himself for a jam. If he gets too close to the tight end as he starts to move or feels threatened from the inside, he pulls off the jam. All that the corner wants to do is make the wide receiver go inside more than he wants. The corner pulls off the jam and positions himself 12-14 yards deep. He gets in a reactive position for a ball being thrown to the corner route or up in the flat. If the corner gets abnormally spaced receivers, he never attempts to move inside. His responsibility is to carry number 2 through the flat to deep. If the two receivers are close to one another, the corner can lose leverage quickly. We don't want to lose leverage deep for the sake of a jam. The safety reads number 2 in the flat. He is responsible for number 1 inside and deep. This is like when the tight end went across.

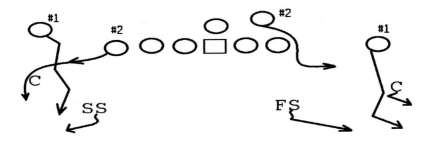

I teach in individual periods route anticipation. I spent some time with the Detroit Lions. That is where I picked this up. I've used it every year and during the season it comes into play. Cut down what you are teaching. If the receiver stems outside and up the field there are two cuts he can make. He can go deep or run the out cut. If the receiver is on the inside and takes an outside release, he can break out or in. If the receiver breaks inside, he can run either break inside or outside. If the receiver breaks across, he can go across or come back. With that in mind, I overlap that with the two-deep coverage for the corners. The corner knows if number 2 is on a vertical and 1 took an outside stem. One can only run the out cut or streak. The corner can keep his eyes where they are supposed to be—on the tight end. He doesn't have to try to sneak a look at the wide receiver. That helps the corner to anticipate what will happen next.

I do a drill that helps in jamming receivers. I'll have a tight end, wide receiver, and quarterback. The tight end and wide receiver are normally spaced. The wide receiver is in between two cones 6 yards wide. The corner positions 2 yards outside the wide receiver. The receiver comes off the line, then breaks to the inside cone or the outside cone. If he breaks in, the corner gets the two-handed jam. If the receiver breaks out, he gets a one-handed jam. I spend more time with the corner than anyone else. I watch his vision, footwork, and his movement. I stand behind the offense so I can see the corner. I watch his eyes, motion, position, and when he jams. If the receiver is inside and in front of the corner, he jams him hard.

The jam is like pass protection for the linemen. We want the butt down. His feet are a little wider than shoulder width. The thumbs are up and he punches with the hands and explodes the upper body into the shoulder area of the receiver. The corner keeps his head back. We don't want to lunge forward. We don't want to get out of balance and twisted. If the receiver releases outside, the corner may get only a one-handed jam. Any one-handed jam is done with the outside hand only. Never try to get the inside hand in the jam. When we jam either hard or one-handed, it is one quick shot. We don't try to ride them. All we are trying to do is knock them off course and in toward the safety. After the jam the vision goes back to the quarterback and he gets ready to react to the thrown ball.

Chapter 8

MAN-TO-MAN
SECONDARY TECHNIQUES

Tom McMahon
University of Wisconsin
1994

I know what coaches say when they hear someone talk about Man-to-Man Coverage. They say, "We do not have the athletes to play man coverage. We can play our athletes on the wide receivers and have success." That is the first thing everyone thinks. I am here to tell you, and I have been coaching the secondary for 18 years, I have never had a situation ever where we did not have great matchups on all wide receivers. I have always been involved with a defense that played man-to-man. We never had the type of players that had the same athletic ability as the wide receivers had, but we were successful.

What we had to do was to come up with some techniques to be able to put our defenders in a position so they could do the job. I want to make this statement to you: Man-to-man coverage is the simplest coverage to put into your defensive package. It is real easy. You take that cat, you take that cat, and you have that cat. It is easy. If you are a corner you go outside and line up on the widest receiver and you play man-to-man. It is easy to get aligned and it is easy to give the players the responsibilities of who to cover. Even in motion situations, it is easy to tell a player if the man goes in motion that way for YOU to take him. It is the easiest defense to get lined up in. The most difficult part is teaching the techniques to get the job done.

If you have the attitude that you are afraid to play Man Coverage you will have trouble. If you are afraid your kids will get beat deep all the time, you will not enjoy playing Man Coverage. When we play Man Coverage the first thing that goes through my mind is not how we match up on the back end, because we know we are not going to have the same type of athletes on the same players. My concern is how good are the outside linebackers and the inside linebackers in applying pressure on the quarterback. Can they put enough pressure on the quarterback so the Bootleg and Play-Action Passes become non-effective passes? I want to know if they can challenge the offensive blocking scheme. I want to know if the offense is sophisticated enough to pick up a run through a linebacker. Can they handle both outside linebackers coming off the edge? Those are the things I want to know when we start talking Man Coverage. I want to know if our linebackers are good at avoiding blocks. Everyone will put a hat on a hat in their scheme. That is not the issue. We want to force the offense to prove they can handle our pressure. Most teams, including high school teams, have a design to pick up three rushers or four rushers. They release five men out on the patterns. Everyone has the ability to protect that scheme. Now, I want to see if you add another rusher, outside or inside, if the offense can pick it up. I want to find that out. My concern is not if we can cover the receivers man-to-man; my concern is if we can cover them long enough. We want to put enough pressure on them to give us time to cover the receivers. I am here to help you overcome any doubt about playing Man Coverage.

Most defensive schemes utilize some form of Man Coverage. Why do you want to use Man Coverage? It is to add additional pressure where you do not have to void a zone. We like to lock up man-to-man and send an extra rusher. I am talking about five or more rushers. We want to get our defenders closer to the receivers they are going to be defending. Most offensive teams try to throw the ball where the defense is not. By playing Man Underneath it allows your defenders to get closer to the intended receivers. Now, you do not have those open zones. When we are in our All-Out Blitz situations, where we are going to come after them, we want more than just to void zones, we want to force the quarterback to hold the ball longer. We do not want him to drop the ball off to a receiver where he can catch the short pass and make a big gain on it before we get to him. So, when we apply seven- and eight-man pressure we are going to come after you. In Red Zone Coverages we know that teams go to individual routes. We know that teams in high school may not change their offense that much in the Red Zone. We want the ability to play Man Coverage where we may want to double cover some wideouts. We will play a little more Man Coverage in the Red Zone. Our theory is that we may gamble a little more. We are going to come at the quarterback to force the offense to keep receivers in for protection. We are going to force the quarterback to get rid of the ball right now, rather than take the sack.

In Combination Man Coverages we can double either wide receiver on each side of the ball. We can take both of them out of the game by having four backs cover two receivers and play Man Coverage Underneath. This gives us a chance to play Man Coverage. We can be a little more risky with the corners knowing they have help behind them. They can play certain routes.

When we get into an Eight-Man Front when a team is utilizing two tight ends, and we want to slide an extra defensive back into a linebackers position, and we have a wide receiver to cover and we want to play a Man scheme, one of the choices we have is to play Man Free Coverage with it. It is difficult to get any of the eight men on defense that are in the box to get outside far enough to help you on wide receivers. They can help you on inside routes, but they are never going to be a factor on outside routes if they are playing inside linebacker. These are the reasons we play Man-to-Man Coverages. I do not think you should be so concerned that there might be mismatches on the coverage.

Everything is related to timing. Before I went to Wisconsin, I was at Arizona State. Coach Alvarez and the staff were doing a great job in getting recruits. The situation with the secondary was this. They had two corners that graduated that went to the Pros. They had real good defensive backs. They did not have many of them but they had some good ones. Their recruiting efforts went to other positions. They were not so concerned about the secondary. They did not recruit any defensive backs. When I was brought into the picture we had two senior corners graduate and no one played behind them. They took every snap for two years. They played a lot of Man Coverage and Man Free defense. That was their scheme. They went Five-Man Pressure, and played Pressure and Man behind the pressure.

When I got into the picture the two players we used at the corners could walk straight under the tables you are sitting at. They were the two best special-team players we had. They were the only two players we had left to play there. Most people think the Big Ten is a smash-mouth football league where you have to defend the run. Our first thought is to defend the run. But, we are looking at some great wide receivers in the Big Ten. My first thought was that we would have to back off the wide receivers to help the small defensive backs. But Coach Alvarez said we are going to go after them and that I would have to get those corners out on the receivers. Since then we have gotten some help from junior colleges and it has helped a great deal. You do not have to have great players to play the corners, but it helps. The thing you must have is a good scheme.

I want to get to three points that will make a difference to you in playing Man-to-Man Coverage. There are three basic factors of Man-to-Man Coverage:

1) The ability of the Receivers. Speed is not the most important factor; the most important factor is the ability to get open. Whether they have speed or not is not the big thing; whether they can get open concerns me more.

2) The quarterback having time to throw the football. You run out of patience when the quarterback faces the four-man rush and he gets the ball away. The offense is playing throw and catch and the defensive backs are playing tackle and the chains are moving. We want to know if their protection scheme will hold out. We want to know if the quarterback will throw the ball accurately when someone is in his face. Some quarterbacks just do not like to be harassed.

3) The Offensive Schemes teams have to use when you play Man-to-Man Coverage. When we talk about the all-out blitz we expect to see the Hot Schemes. We want to know if a team has a hot receiver. You can determine this before you line up. You can let the defenders identify the person the quarterback will try to get the ball to in pressure situations. You will see that most of the time it will be the inside receivers the quarterback goes to in pressure situations. Some teams will sight adjust. They will see a linebacker walked up and the quarterback and wide receiver have a little game going. They will throw the ball outside to the wideout. That is what we call sight adjust. Almost every offense will do that. Some teams use the picks to get receivers open. It can drive you nuts. Some offenses do not run the pick. But some teams use the pick and you have to learn to deal with them.

To counter these factors or to offset them, what do we do? By teaching certain techniques that are best against certain offenses. I will cover them later. Next is Matchups. You have to determine who your best cover man is, and who your second best cover man is. It does not make a lot of difference what his ability is. After that it does not make a lot of difference. Establish who those two guys are and if the offense uses wide receivers, it may be where you want to put your best cover people. If wide receivers go to the same side, you may want to put both of the best defenders to that side. You are matching your best to their best, no matter what ability you may have or they may have. That is one of the things you will have to contend with when you decide you want to play Man-to-Man Coverage. In all

Zone Coverage Schemes the Ball is the issue. You can get a good idea where the ball is going before it ever leaves the hand of the quarterback. In Man Coverage the Receiver is the issue. Never lose sight of this fact. The defender must have his eye on his man and he can't be concerned by anything else.

I want to cover some Basic Rules of Man-to-Man Coverage. If you do not have these things you will never be successful, I do not care how fast your defenders are. Defenders must have these basic things or they will get beat, regardless of how great an athlete they are. These are things I have taken from others that I have been around. I have not come up with anything new. These are common denominators and rules that I have put together.

The Eyes may be the most important factor in Man Coverage. More times than not, when you get beat on a pass is when the defender takes his eye off the receiver. His eyes have to be focused and he has to have a place to watch. He does not want to take a look at the entire body. You can never lose focus, particularly through the break point. The big problem you will have on a receiver running the Out Route will be this. The defender has his eyes on the receiver running his route and all of a sudden he runs an outside route and the defender's eyes go inside. As soon as the defender's eyes leave the receiver through the break point, you are screwed two ways. First, if the receiver does anything off the route, the defender never sees him to make the adjustment. I am talking about a double route such as a Stop and Go. The defender must keep his eyes on the receiver through the break point. The second way it is a problem is this. When the defender's eyes go back inside, the first thing that happens is that the defensive back slows down. He does not go to the point you want him to go. He thinks the ball may be anywhere and he is going to adjust to the ball. That is where you get separation. It seems to be a bigger factor on the outside route because the eyes are back inside away from the receiver. On an inside route the eyes come right back with the receiver and he has an opportunity to look through the receiver and play the football. It is critical when playing Man Coverage that the defender's eyes stay on the receiver. This means to keep your eye on the man all the way through the break point.

I tell our players to take it four steps through the break point. If they will do that they will never see the quarterback throw the ball on an Out Route. They will see it come through a vision by playing the top-side shoulder. Now they can play the ball and step in front of the receiver and make the catch or strip the ball from the receiver. The eyes are the biggest points in Man Coverage. We tell them not to take their eyes off the receiver until they know they have the receiver under control and they are in a position to play that receiver. When they do that they can come up to the ball. I am talking about the Fade and the Takeoff Routes. Never look back to the ball until you have that receiver under control.

Let me tell you how I feel about defensive backs. If they did not have a chance to lift weights, and there was no equipment for them to use during the off-season, I would choose two things to develop defensive backs. First, I would want a jump rope. This is for quick feet. I do not care how fast they are or if they are good athletes. That does not have a lot to do with Man Coverage. I would get them on a jump rope because it all starts with the feet. Don't tell me how fast they are, tell me how quick they move their feet. How quickly do they have the ability to plant their feet and change directions? Our defensive backs live and die on the jump rope and they actually hate it. It is a tough thing to do. I am talking about really getting on the balls of the feet and burning their feet. We want movement of the feet.

The second thing I would do would be to work for Grip Strength or Hand Strength. The feet and the hands are the most important things in developing defensive backs. I would take two five-gallon buckets and fill them three quarters of the way with rice. I would have them dig through the rice to the bottom of the bucket. Then I would have them work their hands back up through the rice. That improves grip strength. You can teach them all of those other things, but I would teach them to move their feet and develop their Grip or Hand Strength.

The ability to close all depends on footwork. I will take you through some drills to show you how we teach footwork. I know you are trying to get all of the other aspects of football taught to your players, and this is more for the players to learn. I understand all of this. We talk about keeping the feet tight at the break point. We talk about keeping proper balance, and keeping our weight under our shoulders, and keeping level, and keeping our shoulders down. We tell them they are always standing on a bubble. When I am talking about the bubble I am talking about having my weight and shoulders over my feet. We want to be able to turn and run with our shoulders down. The biggest problem we have is we have them standing straight up. The next thing they must do is to sink their weight down to make any kind of transition or set weight in their feet to make the break.

Let's talk about Position At The Break point. We identify Break point as 6 yards down the field. I like to talk in terms of steps. We say 12 to 14 steps down the field. We are going to talk about a particular technique. We are going to talk about Off Man and Press Man. Off Man is where you are playing Man Coverage but you are not pressed up tight on the receiver. You play off the receiver at the break point. We tell our players this. It does not have anything to do with the way they initially line up. We will initially align where we want to be at the break point. We tell them where we want them to align based on several things. It may be based on the split of the wide receiver, type of passes we will have to defend, and based on where help will be coming from. We want our guys on the Inside Armpit or on the Outside Armpit depending on the inside or outside technique we play. We give them that point of reference. If I am going to play an Inside Technique and the ball is to my inside, I will take the V of my armpit and the break point is going to be at the V of his armpit, period. End of discussion! That is it. That is where I want to see it. Not only can you get beat over the top, but you can get beat inside or outside. You have to give them a reference point at the break point of where you want them to be to be able to play routes and have an advantage. We do not want to be nose up with the receivers. They want to get you where they have you nose up so they can break either way. We want to have an inside advantage where the receiver has to cross my body to go on an inside route. We may want an outside advantage if we have some inside help. We will tell them where we want them to be and we will check them at the break point. We want to know where they are when the receiver is 6 yards down the field, or 12 to 14 steps down the field.

If it is Full Man Inside there is absolutely no help. We would be blitzing everyone. We would protect the middle of the field. We tell our guys if it is an all-out blitz we want the ball to be thrown deep and outside. We do not want it quick and inside. When there is Zero Coverage and no help, we are going to align one full man shoulders' width to the inside. That is where we are going to be at the break point. We are going to play the Slant and the Post first. You check it out; the home runs come on the Slant or the Post. You can force the quarterback to run out of the pocket, but he should be on his back. If we are going to give anything up, it is going to be an outside route. Even if we are inside and they run a Quick Out, at least we are outside on the man, and we can tackle the man and line up and play again. If you get outrun and get beat to the inside, you have to stretch to see who hits his head on the goal post first. It is not what we want. We are going to take the inside position away. That is when we do not have help inside and we do not have a middle-of-the-field player.

The next thing is Full Man Outside. That is when we are going to Bracket, or we are going to have immediate help to the outside wide receiver. We will be a Full Man to the outside of the different breaking points. We are going to jump hard on everything outside. We are going to take the advantage of the outside route. We are going to be One Full Man Outside with immediate help inside. We would like to see the shoulders square at the break point 12 to 14 steps down the field. Do we always get this? NO! We are not really upset about it. If a receiver closes that cushion, and you are backing up, you can't ask that defender to get the shoulders square when the man is running up his toes. If he runs by you and he hands you a Chapstick as he goes by because he has blistered you, they are going to throw the ball high up in the air and beat your rear end. You can't have them do that. If the receiver turns out, that is fine. As long as he turns out, and we still have the inside armpit, I still make any break that I want to make with my hips turned outside. I do not like that because I would rather see an aggressive backpedal with the shoulders square. But if they turn out, let them turn out and then we will go from there.

When I say Feet Tight this is what I am talking about: At the breaking point is where you get beat. When you are playing Man-to-Man Coverage you do not want the feet to be out wide; not to be stepped back, but you want the feet underneath the inside of the crotch. You want to take the normal backpedal. Watch the defender when he makes his stop. The first thing he does is to widen his feet. When he moves his feet wider and has to go in any direction he doesn't have the push that he needs. He has to keep both feet under his crotch so he can keep his feet down and his weight on the balls of his feet and he can push off in any direction. He can't have his feet spread wide. He needs to keep his feet tight.

We talk about Shoulder Weight. If the weight comes up, the first thing they are doing is to struggle to get back and they struggle to keep separation and their shoulders come up. Nine times out of 10 they have to drop their shoulders down and forward to get any kind of break. We want to keep the shoulders low until the break. Even if they are opening and running we want the shoulders down because they may have to break off that turn.

Let me talk about focal point. I have talked about eyes and I have talked about getting the eyes on the target to cover the man. I tell my players it is like a batter facing Nolan Ryan with his eyes closed. He will never hit the baseball. The eyes are important, but where do you put your eyes? If you are playing an Inside Technique and you are playing Off Man, our eyes go to the Belt Buckle to his inside hip.

That is all I want them to see. If he is playing the Outside Technique I want them to see the Belt Buckle to the outside hip. That is what it tells the defensive back. It tells him when to anticipate a receiver is going to break. So many kids want to look at the upper torso. The first thing the receiver coach tells his players is to make an inside Pin move. Well, that doesn't do anything to the belt or the hip, but the defensive man moves. The belt does not drop and the hip does not disappear. They want to look at the receiver's face. That is not going to help them when they play Man Coverage.

As far as the cushion is concerned we must ask this question: How far do you tell a defensive back to get off a receiver to keep from getting beat? He still must be able to break back to the football. A lot of this has to do with the defensive back's speed. It is a fill for the defensive back. He has to know when he should open his hips. If you have backs with average speed you want him 2 yards from that 6-yard break point. The base is 2 yards. If the back is faster we may say that it is 1½ yards if you have good speed. If you have a player who can really open and run and you want to squeeze the receiver you can play him at 1 yard. We use that as a change-up.

The purpose of Man-to-Man Coverage is not just to cover the man but to prevent the completion. We want to make the interception. You have to make great decisions on how to do this. We had 23 interceptions this year, which led the Big Ten. I am proud of that fact because we only had 12 the year before that. Half of those interceptions came on Man-to-Man Coverage. That tells me you can intercept the ball in Man or Zone. If you can't get the interception we want to knock the ball down and knocked out of the area. It ain't over until it is over. If we do not have a chance to get two hands on the ball, we want to grab the ball. If you have to leave your feet and do not get the ball, be aware. You may have big-time problems. If you can only put one hand on the ball, let's knock it down. In order to do this you must have good position.

It does not stop when we are playing Man when a man catches the ball. It will only stop when we have made a play to try to knock the ball out of his hand to get a fumble, or we strip the ball from the receiver's hand. If the receiver catches the ball and does not put it away we want to strip the ball. We want to *Paw* the ball. This happens at every level. A receiver will catch the pass and a back will come over and try to knock the ball out of the receiver's hands with only one hand. If he misses the ball the receiver makes a long gain out of the play. The key is to use two hands to strip the ball, always.

We want them to always have a knock-through hand and a secure hand. The only thing we do is a knock-through and a secure move. Both hands have to work when you are going to knock the ball out of the receiver's hand.

The next thing is to make the tackle. We want the tackle up high. We want the tackle hard and we want to try to knock the ball out. If the first man is not there to knock the ball out, the second man goes for the ball. The second man always comes in with the thought process that he is going to knock the ball out.

The last thing we want to do is tackle the man if we miss the ball. We do not want to let him run with it after the catch. We do not want a long gain. We tell the man if he gets out of position not to stop and look for the ball. We want him to get back as quickly as he can and then make the tackle. Don't worry about the fact that you have been outrun and have been beaten; get back and make the tackle. Let's line up and play again. Don't give up the big play. It doesn't have to be all bad.

You can always establish contact. You can establish your physical presence, and you have to. Your people have to hit people in the mouth. If you have a receiver that is intimidated you can tell the defenders to go high instead of going low for the ball. Go through his face mask. That is where the big hits come from. If you are a small ant, hit someone in the mouth if you want to get his attention. Hit them up high and don't worry about how big they are.

When you are playing Man inside the Red Zone, or inside the 12-yard line, when they are going to score, you never play Man-to-Man Coverage on the top side. You never play it on the topside shoulder when you are backed up to the 12-yard line. You play all of your Man Coverage when you are underneath the receiver. You want to make the ball go through you to get to the receiver. How many times have you seen it when the defender had great coverage behind or on the top side and the receiver made a great catch? The defender tackles the receiver in the end zone. What good does that do? Make him come up and play underneath the wide receiver. Make the ball go through the defender to get to the receiver. Now, if there is a scramble, have the defender turn and face the receiver just like he would if he were guarding him in basketball. That man is his responsibility.

The defensive back should leave his feet in the end zone. Whatever it is, let it all out in the end zone. When the ball comes to the end zone it is sellout time and you have to go all out to stop the completion.

Get the ball any way you can. Knock it down if you can, but don't stand there when the receiver goes up for the ball. You have to tell your players about this.

Never give up. How many times have you seen a player get beat in practice and just stop going after the receiver? That is when you have to jump his ass. If you get beat or you fall down, you had better get up in a heartbeat and catch back up or you will catch it from the coaches. I do not care how bad you get beat or how bad you look, get up and get back and finish the play. *Finish The Play*. Don't allow them to kick the turf and throw a fit. That will not help anyone. It will be a learned response if you do it to the first man that gets beat and quits on the play. Get in his face and make sure he knows what to do.

Let me get into techniques. I want to cover Stance and Keys. I want to talk about Off Man where we are going to clue the quarterback with a quick step. We want the shoulders square with the eyes on the quarterback on the quick set. That is what we look at to start with. When we get off with the receiver we want to maintain that armpit and shoulder position. We are going to be inside the break point and we are going to focus the eyes on the belt buckle to the inside hip. We have an inside-out relationship at the break point. We have talked about all of this. Now, lets talk about where we are now.

Let's start out by looking at the Quarterback. We clue the quarterback. The kids have to understand what you are trying to do. This is what we use with our corners on wide receivers to start out with. We are going to play Off Man. If we are going to play Off Man and clue the quarterback, we are going to back the defender up to 6 or 7 yards. When I say clue the quarterback this is what I am talking about. The defender's vision is on the quarterback. His High Beam is on the quarterback and his Low Beam is on the receiver. I want to look inside at the quarterback, but in my peripheral vision I can see that receiver as a spot. I want to backpedal out real easy and I clue the quarterback first. Here is the theory behind that. We clue the quarterback for a Three-Step Drop. If he sets up on a Three-Step Drop we know he is going to throw the ball much sooner. We start our backpedal but we start to settle when the quarterback sets up on three steps. We do not drop as fast if he stops at 3 yards. That quarterback will get back to set up at three steps quicker than the receiver will get down the field 6 yards. If he goes back to six steps to set up we haul ass to get back and get set to play the receiver. We do not want a lot of separation between the receiver and defender. The key is this: Once that quarterback sets, the defender must get his eyes back on his receiver as quickly as possible. He can't see the quarterback throw the ball. If he sees the quarterback throw the ball he will not be able to cover the wide receiver.

OFF MAN - CLUE QB

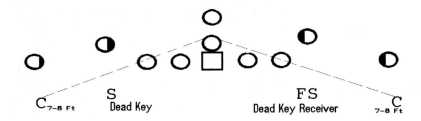

It is the same thing for the Outside Corner to either side. I think you can do this in high school, but you have to work on it. The biggest problem you will have is that the defender will not want to get his eyes back on the receiver. If you have a problem with this I would not play it that way. You tell the defender to put his eyes on the quarterback for the first three steps. If the quarterback stops he looks for the receiver and plays it tough. If the quarterback drops back to six steps or more he must bring his eyes back around and look for the receiver as soon as he knows it is not a Three-Step Drop anymore. The big problem in Off Man is the separation. We tell our players this. If we are in Off Man, whether we are clueing the quarterback or the wide receiver, the big problem is when the receiver catches the ball and turns his shoulders upfield to put a move on a run. That is the worst thing that can happen to you. We tell our players they have to be good enough to be able to attack that wide receiver when he catches the football on either a Spot Route or an Out Route or a Slant Route. You have to be good enough as soon as the receiver turns his shoulder upfield to stick your face in his face to stop him from going upfield. Don't let the man get turned upfield. That is the big problem you have in playing Off Man. The thing that helps us cut down on separation is being able to clue the quarterback.

If we are playing Man on inside receivers this is what we tell them. This includes our Free Safety. Inside defenders cannot clue the quarterback on the Three-Step Drop. This is especially true on Zero Coverage or on a Blitz. They have to Dead Key the wide receivers. This is what I mean by Dead Key: Take both of your eyes and put them on the receiver as soon as the ball is snapped. On a Three-Step Drop the ball will get to the inside receiver a lot quicker. The rule is this: Clue the quarterback if it is a Split Wide Receiver, and Dead Key the Receiver if he is in close to the quarterback for a quick throw.

OFF MAN - ALL DEAD KEY

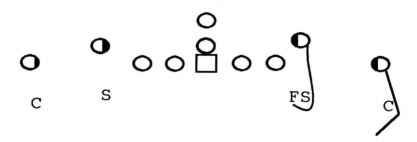

When you want to teach Man-to-Man Coverage you choose the way you want to teach it. I just told you the way we try to get it done. I have a hard time getting them to get their eyes back on the receivers. I will tell you that.

The other way to cover them is to flat-out Dead Key the receivers. When we Dead Key a receiver we will tighten him up a little. He will get off when the receiver starts out. He is looking at the receiver completely and everyone else in the world is dead as far as he is concerned. The defender must react to everything the receiver does. He can't see the Three-Step Drop. He is focused on the wide receiver all of the way. I am not sure if this is not the best way to start out teaching Man Coverage.

We have advantages and disadvantages for playing each type of coverage. If you are playing Off Man and clueing inside to the quarterback you have a better opportunity for the defensive back to help on run support. He could possibly see a run develop. If he is in a Dead Key, the defender must see off the receiver to determine if he is a blocker before he can help on the run. Also, if you are playing inside and the ball is thrown quick and away from you, you can get off your man and go to the ball. When you are Dead Keying a wide receiver, if he turns and runs back to the outside, you are useless in run support. If you have it set up, you will not need him anyway. About the only way that defender can tell if the ball is coming toward him is if the crowd yells if it is an away game and the back makes a big run.

The other technique I want to talk about is the Press Technique. We will mix the Press up. What we mean by Press is this: We are going to get up and take the working room away from the wide receiver.

We want to take the open space away from the receiver. The way we like to do it is to Jump into our Press. We do not want to show Press because we do not want to invite the deep pass. We do not want to show Press because you are never a factor in run support. The receivers are going to run you off. You have to live with that fact. Sometimes we will Press the inside receiver and sometimes we will Press the outside receiver. We will use the Press against teams that like to run the Pick on us. If the receivers do cross we can fight over the top of the pick. We will use Press if we want the quarterback to hold the ball a little more.

We will run the Press if we want to harass a receiver. We teach the Press squared up. We start out shoulder to shoulder. We will assume an Inside or Outside crotch position once we get there. We are going to have our players in a hit position. We are in a hitting position with the weight on the balls of the feet, and the shoulders are square. They check the outside to make sure nothing is past the line of scrimmage. The first thing they must do when the ball is snapped is to look at the receiver. They must be patient. They will bounce their feet. The receiver will make a move; just be patient. Bounce the feet. Now the receiver makes an inside or outside release. Now he wants to put his hands on the receiver. He puts the outside hand on the receiver first on an outside release. We punch the inside hand first on an inside release. We follow up with a two-hand punch always. We want to get our hands on the receiver. Then we work to a hip position.

We will Press with any of our defensive backs. The plays you have to play on the Press are two routes. First is the Fade Route, where they take the ball and throw it over the top. I look at the quarterback to see if he can throw that route. I have seen some quarterbacks who could never complete that pass if no one was out there on defense. That is when we want to Press. You have to be good at playing the Fade Route.

The other route you must be good against is the Slant. The hard outside release and the receiver working back underneath you. It may just be up the field and the receiver comes back underneath you. You can react to the other routes. You work on the Fade and the Slant.

A lot of people think because you play a Press Technique you are going to be playing a Trail Technique. A Trail Technique is when you are behind the receiver and on his inside hip pocket. That is a Trail. When we Press, unless we are playing with help over the top, we will not play a Trail Technique. We will play side by side and lock on the hip. I want to be just behind him where I can still see his front number. I am almost parallel with the man. In his hip pocket, I am underneath the receiver and there is someone over the top. In a regular Press I lock on to him and run down the field like Siamese twins. I do not want to be underneath. I want to be at least even.

Now you have all of the techniques. This is what I mean when we Curl up to a Press. The key is this. We will go to an inside or an outside foot alignment. We take the position that will give us an advantage on either an inside or an outside alignment. Usually for us it is determined by the split of the wide receiver. If the receiver is in tight, the working room is going to be outside. We are going be knee to crotch to the outside. If the man is lined up where we think the working room is to the inside, we would play just the opposite. If we have a receiver pinned on the boundary, we will play him to the inside.

This is an overview of our Off Man and Press Coverages. Now let me cover some drills. First is the Dead Key. We start on a sideline and work to the hash mark. We have them line up on the outside of him and have the receiver come off the line at half speed. We have four or five spread across the line and work all of them at one time. We go half speed and teach all of the techniques we are working on for that practice. The defender lines up at 4 yards and gets on the outside hip to start out with. We want them to understand that when that receiver gets off the line the defender must get off the line. They both have to get off at the same time. We want them to keep a 2-yard cushion. We can check the eyes on the drill and see what they are looking at. You can work them four at a time.

DEAD KEY

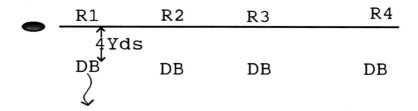

Next we have them run the Dead Weave. We have four receivers working on four defenders. Now, we tell the receiver to take two steps straight ahead to start out with and then to weave to his right or left. They will run into each other. They all are going to go for two steps and then they are going to weave. Now we are working on the approach. The receiver is not going to run straight ahead. They will run to get the defender nose up. But we do not want to be even; we want the advantage of being on the inside or on the outside. We want the defenders to keep the shoulders square in the weave. We do not want the defender to cross over. We want them to backpedal and keep the shoulders down. They must maintain that armpit position.

WEAVE DEAD KEY

Next, we want them to learn to settle at the Break Point. We always have a ball for the receivers to line up on. The command for the receivers to go is simple—Set, Go. I am going to have the receivers start out running and then settle down like they are going to make a break. They are going half speed. The shoulders come down and the hips stay square and the belt buckle stays square. I have the receivers exaggerate coming down on the break.

SETTLE AND BREAK

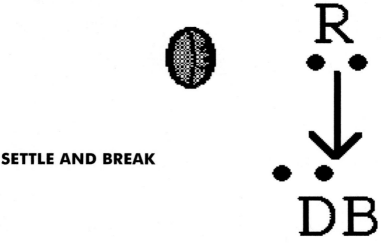

When the defender sees that break he maintains that same cushion and backpedals, and when he sees the break he settles his shoulder weight but keeps moving his feet backward. It is not stopping, it is settling the feet. They are going to settle to get ready to break.

We are teaching defenders how to read receivers at the break point. You can't just talk about it, you have to show them.

Next is what happens on the Takeoff Route. Again, we start out 4 yards off the receiver. Now, the receiver picks up the pace a little. We are looking at the same armpit. Now the receiver crosses my face. I must turn and hook the hip and get next to him. They run together down the field. I am going to take away the inside half of his body and lean him out of bounds. We do that to the left side and then to the right side.

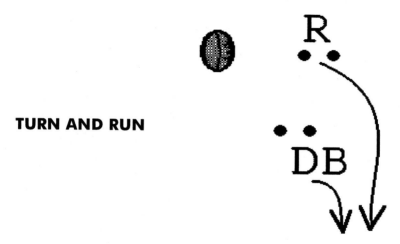

TURN AND RUN

Last is the Catch. What happens when a receiver runs up on the toes on the defender? If we feel we are going to get beat, he will come up and Catch the receiver. We want him to keep his feet moving on the Catch. The Catch is not knocking the crap out of the receiver.

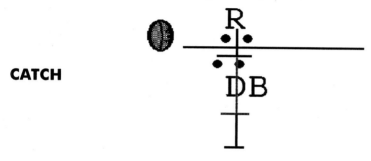

CATCH

If you catch and miss, the receiver gets away. We tell the defender to mush into him. This is not the time to try to knock him down. We want to get in front of him and slow him down. We mush into him and keep our feet moving. If the cushion is broken, we settle and catch the receiver.

Next is Playing The Routes. This is simple defense. I do not have time to run this against the offense. I get two of our guys and we have one on offense and one on defense. I tell the receiver to run an Out or whatever route we are working against. I tell them what I want and that is it. I want to see their footwork on that route. The receiver runs the route and I check the footwork of the defender. There is no guesswork on the play. We run the Out first and then we run the Square-In, and then a Stop Route would be third. We go over all of the routes and work on them.

The second part of the drill is to include the quarterback. Now we work against the Three-Step Drop. Then we go to the Five-Step Drop. It is a teaching progression on defense.

What do you tell a defensive back when he gets beat? "You got beat!" No! You have to tell him more than that. We work on the Press Technique head up. We take the receivers and work on their techniques. All I am looking for at first is the good feet, the good punch, and the hook and the hip to start out with. We take the receivers and just run them down the field. Then we throw the ball and have them play the ball. I used to throw the ball with some degree of accuracy. If I am not throwing it very well, I will tell them the ball is in the air and when I call "Ball" the receiver puts out his arms as if he were catching the ball.

What do you tell the defender if the ball is thrown short? The receiver will put the breaks on and the defensive back is still going. We tell the defender if the receiver turns and gives you both shoulders it is a short pass. When we see both shoulders turn we come back to look for the football. It is a free ball. We are not going to let him come through us to get the ball. When we lock hips we want to always lock the inside half of the player. Play it to the inside half.

I want to draw up some schemes for you. First is our Man Free. We always start out with Four Across when we can. We move the alignments right now or with the cadence. We lock up on the three wide receivers. We will play a lot of this on first down. We see a lot of Play-Action Passes and Bootleg Passes.

MAN FREE

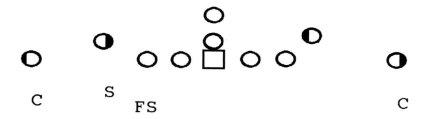

C S FS C

If possible we like to show Four Across. We like to show a Two-Deep Shell. If you play Two Deep it may be good for you. We are going to play Man Free out of Two Deep. Nothing changes for the Mike and Eagle linebackers. Both the Safeties are now going to fill the alley. They are primary alley run support players. We are going to Banjo the Tight End. If we get any run action toward the Strong Safety, regardless of what the Tight End does, the Strong Safety has run support and the Free Safety has the Tight End. We are going to Banjo the Strong Safety. On any outside routes by the Tight End the Strong Safety takes the Tight End. On any routes down the field the Strong Safety takes the Tight End and the Free Safety ends up free. On any Crossing Routes by the Tight End the Free Safety Man takes him and the Strong Safety ends up being free. We are just running the Banjo on the Tight End.

BANJO

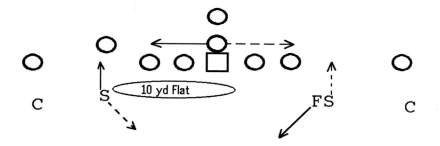

The problem we have to decide on the Banjo is this. If the End runs a Hole Route, who has him? They can't leave the Tight End open in the middle of the field. We designate our Strong Safety to take him on a Hole Route. Safeties stand at 10 yards and are flat-footed. They do not back up. They are alley run players. They play pass if the Tight End comes out.

If you are in Twin Formations you have to make a decision on matchups. If my corners are my best cover men I use them. If the Safeties are the best cover guys we use them. I have done it both ways. If you bring both corners to one side you have to teach the inside corner to play a Three-Deep Zone. You don't want to always bring your corners over because they will know you are in Man. You can bring your corners over and play Zone. You can do it one time and it keeps them off balance.

If we did not want to bring both Corners over to cover Twins we would have our Strong Safety cover one of the two men. Our rule was to allow the Safeties to bump the Corners outside; Corners could never bump Safeties out. If we have both Corners on the Twins and the man went in motion, we would call Lock and Run. If we have a Corner on a wide receiver we stay with him. We call that Lock. If we want both Corners to cover Twins or Two Receivers to one side, we just call it Cover One - Flip.

If we have a wide receiver go in motion you can't Press him anymore. What you have to do is to slide along with him and let him work to your outside just a little. You want to take an inside-out position on him. You do not want him to come underneath you. You want to force him to the outside. Keep your eyes on the man. Never get in to a backpedal with him. All you want to do is to shuffle with him.

When we call Zero Blitz that means we are going to send everyone. We send eight men. We run it two ways. We walk up and show that we are coming, but we won't go. Then we call Mask and go. That means we are playing Four Across and playing Man and the linebackers go. We usually Lock when we run Zero Blitz.

Chapter 9

KEYS FOR COACHING DEFENSIVE BACKS

Dick Moseley
University of Northern Iowa
1994

I've been at Northern Iowa for a year and a half. I'm the new kid on the block. I really like Minnesota. I recruited 4 kids out of here last year. Northern Iowa uses Minnesota athletes and they do well. We are a I-AA school. I have spoken at these Coach of the Year Clinics three times. The first time I spoke I was the Defensive Coordinator for Cal Stoll. Some of you guys weren't even around when I coached at Minnesota. We were at Minnesota as a staff from 1972-79.

I know a lot of you guys know Buck Nystrom. For you younger guys, that is your loss. I liked him. I coached with him at the University of Colorado. I knew him when he was playing for Cal at Michigan State. Buck will probably go down as one of the best offensive line coaches that has ever coached the game on any level. He has since retired. Back then he was a volatile clinic speaker. He was probably the most demanding clinician going, in terms of the offensive line.

One year I was sitting on the front row for his lecture. He saw me and called me up on the stage to help him demonstrate. He beat the crap out of me for an hour and a half on the stage. He was demonstrating the club, rip, and other techniques on me. He left and I got up to speak. Everyone started to walk out because they figured there was not much left of me.

I've always believed you have to have confidence in your ability. You have to have confidence in your ability as a player and coach. I went to the Senior Bowl a couple of weeks ago. It is sponsored by the NFL. It is a big deal. I went and I was at a hospitality session rubbing elbows with some big-name people. I was talking to a pro player who had come to the game by way of a celebrity golf outing in Florida. This guy was from Boston. Being from Boston he was teamed up with Ted Williams, the baseball commissioner, and another big name.

After the match they were all sitting around talking. Someone asked Ted how he would do today hitting against today's pitchers. Today they have all of those special guys on the roster. They have short relievers and long relievers. "What do you think you would hit today, Ted?" He told them maybe .270 or .275. Everyone began to look at the ground to try to figure why he was so conservative. Finally, he said, "Guys give me a break, I'm 75 years old." That is confidence in your ability.

The next thing I want to talk about is visualization. The theme of the book I read on visualization was "man can achieve only what he can conceive." I was a Detroit city kid. I went to Detroit Central High School. We had 500 kids in our graduating class. When I was a senior, our commencement exercises were held in a hot auditorium. We had a guy from Wayne State University to deliver the address. We were 17 years old. We were hot, wearing caps and gowns. We just wanted to get out of that stove. This speaker came out with a big jar of white beans. I couldn't believe it. He reached in his pocket and pulled out a great big walnut. He took the top off the jar and put the walnut down to the bottom of this jar full of beans. He continued to talk but no one was listening. They were watching him shake the jar of beans. Of course the walnut was working it's way to the top of that jar every time he shook it. When it got to the top he jammed it back down to the bottom again. I was watching this guy and thinking he was crazy because I was hot and wanted out of this place. He did this four or five times while he was addressing our class. How many of you sitting in here today can remember what your commencement speaker's theme was? None of you can. This is what visualization is all about. This guy finally told us after he had brought that walnut up from the bottom of the jar about five times. "You can't keep a good man down." I remembered that theme, but I didn't remember anything else that man said that day.

There is a place for visualization in high school football. Visualization can come in many forms. It could be posters on the wall, slogans and goals posted, or any number of things. I coached with the Packers. I remember one slogan when I was there. It was posted on the wall. "The strength of the pack is the wolf, and the strength of the wolf is the pack." Every time I read that slogan, even being an old coach today, I say "Yes!" That is not all of the answer, but there are a lot of things you can do with visualization. Many of them can be excellent motivating factors.

I like the story about Roger Banister. He was the first guy to run a sub-four-minute mile. For years people tried to break the four-minute mile, but no one could do it. Roger broke the barrier in 3:59.2. Six months later a guy from Australia by the name of John Landy ran the mile in 3:58. He brought that time down. Less than 12 months later an 18-year-old kid from Australia named Herb Elliot ran it in 3:56.6 and the whole world was taken aback. This was all happening in less than a two-year period, when for centuries it could not be done. Less than a year later a kid from Kansas by the name of Jim Ryun ran it in 3:51.5. What are we saying here? When you die they will still be breaking records. No one has ever lived where they are not breaking records. In 1936 a guy by the name of Johnny Weissmuller won five gold medals in the 1936 Olympics. He was the hero of the world. Today 12-year-old girls are swimming faster than he did in the 1936 Games.

High school coaches have no idea of the influence they have on a kid. They may come from a broken home with no father image. Don't let those types of kids slip under the rug. Well, that is my philosophical stuff I brought here.

Let me talk about football. In a National Convention in 1964, Ara Parseghian of Notre Dame showed us the SAKRAT Rule. The first letter is a progression of teaching. They stand for *Stance*, *Alignment*, *Key*, *Responsibility*, *And Technique*. That could be either side of the ball. The same thing would hold true for the offense as well. If you can wake this kid up at 3 a.m. and ask him to give you his SAKRAT rule for a certain coverage and he can do it, you are giving him a chance to win.

I want to go over "Cover 1," which is "Man-Free" with you. It doesn't matter what type of front you run. As soon as you establish the fact that you have four rushers, the other guys make up the coverage. For the diagram, let's look at a stack defense with a "Cover 1." People play the Cover 1 when they want to pressure the offense. A pressure defense to me is when you send five rushers. Here we are going to bring two linebackers up the middle. We are going to match up with corners on wide receivers, outside linebackers on the backs, and strong safety on the tight end. The free safety is free.

There are two big plays that the offense tries to run against Man Free. The first one is called the "Bend-In." This is a shallow cross usually run by the tight end, or hard post cut, usually run by the flanker. The split end is running the window underneath at 17 yards. In Cover 1, the flanker runs a hard post through the free safety. The corners play a tight outside eye forcing the man to the free safety, who is playing for the post.

BEND-IN VS. COVER 1

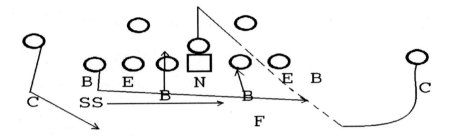

The offense has taken your post player out of coverage with the hard post. The corner on the split-end side is playing the same technique because he has the free safety playing the post. But the free safety is helping on the post cut of the flanker. The split end runs a Square-In at 17 yards and the window opens up and the offense converts on the pass. The defense has done nothing wrong, but they still lose.

The second play that can hurt the Cover 1 is the Dig Route. Let's do the same thing only this time take the split end to the post. The free safety's rule is to take all deep post cuts. Now the other two receivers are going to go down to 17 yards and run a Dig or Square-In. The corner and strong safety are holding hard on the outside thinking they have help from the free safety on the inside. If everything is equal, the offense will win again even though the defense has done nothing wrong.

DIG VS. COVER 1

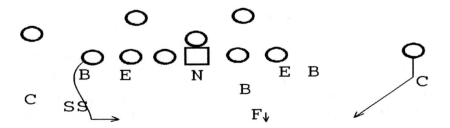

Let's look at the same thing but change what we have to change. The corners are going to hold a hard inside eye alignment. The free safety has no change. The free safety is still run out of the play. But, the corner is holding a hard inside eye, which gives him a chance if all things are equal, to stop the play on the Dig or Bend-In. Now, the Bend-In and the Dig Route are no longer the plays the offense wants. Don't change your free safety's role just because he is in Cover 1. He may or may not be able to help, depending on what the offense runs. What I am saying is all man coverage should be played with a hard inside eye technique. He should stay 3 yards off and 1 yard inside the receiver as he takes his vertical upfield route.

The next thing you tell your kids is that he is going to be a one-way player. Give the defense the advantage. Everything tells us the offense has the advantage. The receiver is running forward and knows where he is going. The defensive backs have to take away everything to the inside. Any inside move by the receiver, the defensive back is driving hard on it. If the receiver takes the outside move, the defensive back reacts to that move. His motor is running but he is not driving on the move.

If the coach tells his defensive back to deny all inside cuts and react to all outside, he has given the defensive back an advantage. He is playing recovery football to anything on the outside, but the odds are in his favor. On an 8-yard Out Route all the odds come to the defensive back. The distance of the throw, flight of the ball, boundary, and the margin of error is in the defense's favor.

The problem is how you have coached the defensive back. You have coached him to drive on the inside move. When the receiver runs the hard post cut and turns to the corner route, the defensive back has to have sound technique. He is going to do what you have coached him to do. He breaks on the inside cut. The receiver comes off the pattern and turns for the corner. The defensive back's hips are turned and he is running. This is where the defensive back has to have worked on the center-field turn, and turn quick back to the pattern.

You should not coach a defensive back one day without a quick-turn drill. That is where the defensive back rips his head and shoulders around, drives on the ball, gains every advantage he can on the air time, gets to the interception point, and makes a play on the ball. The thin Post Corner takes time.

The message here is to coach your Man Coverage the same regardless of what type of scheme you are running. The same means take away the inside. Take the 3 and 1 cushion inside and hope you can maintain your backpedal. If you lose that cushion, turn your hips and run to the inside. If the guy runs the thin post, always be ready for the post corner. If you don't play like that, you give the receiver a two-way go on the defensive back.

Football is a game of the progression of logic. I'll tell you how simple that is. You can take any offensive play that you want and it will be successful until you give me the chalk. Once you give me the chalk I can stop your play. The next thing you will say is, "Give me that chalk, because I'm going to run it over here." What I'm saying is football is a game of the progression of logic of who has the chalk last. There are only 22 guys out there. It's not like going to the moon. It is simple.

Great football coaches are boring. They teach their kids everything there is to know about football. They have blitz packages, short-yardage packages, goal-line packages, third-and-long packages, and a package for every situation there is. When your kids get so bored they can say they don't care what they do; we can play, that is what you are looking for. None of us gets to that position but we try.

Think about this. If, in fact, you have bored that kid to where he can never make a mistake, he can truly play anything you ever wanted to play. He truly has the stance, alignment, key, responsibility, and technique. He knows everything you know to teach him. You bombard him with repetition until he is totally bored. When that happens, you have to allow that guy to play with absolute reckless abandon within the system of the defense. That's when you have a chance to win.

Let's talk about creativity as a football coach. I am just a grass-roots, toolbox, blue-collar coach. That's all I am. I work at it like you do. Take this phrase: creativity versus plagiarism. Don't worry about being a visionary. Don't worry about being a creative genius. I learned that from Bear Bryant. He told me he never had an original thought in his life. But he could take your thoughts and coach them better than you could. He meant that.

Chapter 10

THE OSU 4-3 SECONDARY COVERAGES

Fred Pagac
Ohio State University
1996

I am going to talk about our Secondary Coverages at Ohio State. Basically I want to talk about how we tie our secondary and linebackers together on our coverages in our two basic schemes or packages. I will talk about Cover 2 and Cover 4, which is Quarters and Halves.

When we talk about Ohio State defensive football, we basically play two different fronts. We play what we call the Tight Eagle Package, which is the reduced package on the split-end side. We play the 1 and 5 techniques to the tight-end side. We also play the 4-3 Stack, which we have been playing for about six years now. The third front that we play is more of a man type in which we go to our 4-6 package. Today I will cover our Base Coverages: Cover 2 and Cover 4. We are going to play these two coverages about 75 percent of the time.

The thing we are trying to accomplish first is this: We are going to come out and play a shell Cover 2. That is our 4-Deep Scheme with our Linebackers involved in the coverage. We want to be able, by the disguise of game play, to show either Cover 3 or Soft Coverage, and then be able to play both coverages out of that look. If we are playing a hard corner Cover 2 that particular week, we may be showing Soft Coverage on the snap of the ball and then step to the hard corner. We will play this out of our Stack Front, and out of our Tight Front, which we call Tight Eagle.

When we get into the two different schemes we teach them two different principles. We teach a Cloud Principle to the front side of the ball, which means the frontside triangle. We also teach the Cloud

Principle to the backside triangle. When we do that we are playing Cover 2. We are going to play 5 Underneath, and we are going to play 2 Deep. It is a progression defense. We talk about collision of receivers, and we talk about taking away verticals, and getting back on the ball, and playing leverages over receivers, and breaking on the ball.

If we are going to play Cover 4, which is straight quarters, we are going to teach a Read Principle. When we teach the Read Principle we are talking about those same triangles. The safeties will communicate what the support scheme is. He will call out "Read—Read—Read" or "Cloud—Cloud—Cloud." He calls out what they are playing. When they make the call they are talking to those three people in the triangle. They are talking about both Run Support and Pass Coverage.

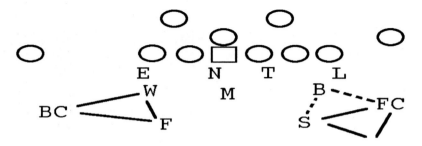

To tie this in we need to look at our secondary alignments. Our corners are going to be between 7 and 9 yards deep. It is the same alignment if we are playing Cover 2 or 4. Our safeties are going to be lined up 10 to 12 yards deep. As far as width is concerned, we do try to cheat with them as far as ability alignment is concerned. If we are playing a Read Principle they will be aligned a little tighter. If we are playing a Cloud Support they will be a little wider and more toward the hash mark.

The linebackers listen for their calls. We are going to communicate with them by hand signals. If we are playing Cloud Support, it means we are playing Cover 2 to that half of the ball. Linebacker-wise, we tell them this: They are to play the run and react to the pass on most plays. On third-and-long they will look for the pass first. The secondary players play the pass and react to the run. If you are a primary support player you are going to support the run first and pass second.

If we get a Cloud call to the tight end, this is how we play it. To the tight-end side of the ball we have Cloud Support. If the offense runs the option to the tight-end side, this is how we play it. Our first rule is this: our linebackers key flow. The Will linebacker is looking through the near guard to flow; the Mike linebacker is keying flow to the guard the flow goes to. The Buck backer is going to check flow. His first responsibility is to get his eyes in the "C" Gap tunnel and find out what the tight end is doing. On Cover 2, if pass shows, or we get flow coming to the Buck backer, he must step to the "C" Gap and find out what is happening. On passing action he will see the tackle sitting back off the line soft, and he will see the tight end coming up through the seam. On Cover 2 we ask the Buck to knock the crap out of the tight end.

Let me talk about Run Responsibilities. If I am a frontside linebacker and get action toward me, I am going to check the tunnel. If it opens, we are going to run through it. We never discourage a run-through. If I am a backside linebacker and the action goes away, I want to step up and check my secondary key, whether it be the guard or tight end, depending on which side I am on. I must hold for the Cutback before I flow. We probably play the Stack a little slower than most teams do. The reason for that is because of the Cutback play.

Next is the Run Responsibilities for the Secondary. Our secondary will key ball flow. They want to know if the ball is on the line of scrimmage or off the line of scrimmage. They look at the different angles for the ball. They want to know if it is Drop-Back, Sprint, or Ball on the Line action. If we were to get the option to the tight end, our corner would be the support player. Our strong safety is going to play pass 1. For the Buck backer, if the alley or "C" Gap opens, he will run through. If the alley closes, he will collision 2. If 2 is arcing, Leo should knock the crap out of him to give the safety time to get into field position. Our bench corner, with the action going away, should be in a Soft Sink, insurance position. Everyone else is going to fill lanes, inside out.

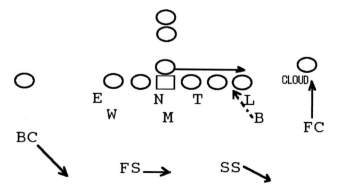

Now we will look at a Read Call. The difference in a Read Call and a Cloud Call is this: the corner to the Read Side is going to be playing basically a Man Technique. We are going to show Cover 2. The corner will have the 1 receiver to his side in a Man Technique on any route that is run over a 10-yard area. That area could be flexible according to what you are seeing each game. That area could be 8 yards or it could be 12 yards. We tell the corner if the ball comes up the field in a vertical manner and he is in a Man Technique, then he must weave to an inside-out leverage position. We know if we are playing a Read Support system on a Passing Game, then our weakness will be on the Out routes. Now, we know the quarterback still has to complete those passes. The receivers still must make those catches, but we know that area is our weak spot. If they make the completion we will make the tackle.

If by chance we happen to make an interception on an out route, we may pat the corner on the back, and at the same time we may kick him in his rear end because we do not want him to get beat on a deep post route. If he gets beat deep later on, it is his fault. He must deny the post route and all deep routes.

The big reason this defense has evolved, even with the Cowboys and Chicago Bears, is to get run support. They want their safeties stepping down. On any type of Run Action, the safety is going to sit and flat-foot read. Nothing changes up front. As far as Option or Run Responsibilities, nothing has changed. Nothing changes with the front seven. They play it the same way. The support comes from the safety. Anything else off the ball side we play it the same way. The corner will always be late support on anything going away.

Our Base Coverage is 2 and 4. If, by chance, we are getting hurt on a Weak-Side Post Route, we have the ability with our Cover System to go to Cover 6. We teach our players two things on our coverages. The frontside corner, the Buck backer, and the strong safety are taught Cloud and Read Techniques. The same is true on the back side. The Will backer, the boundary corner, and the free safety are taught Cloud and Read Techniques. If we are getting the Frontside Post Action and we want to get a half player on the back side, all we have to do is to go to Cover 6. That is the old coverage of quarter, quarter, half. That gives us Cover 2 on the back side and Cover 4 on the front side. That is our Cover 6.

If we are getting hurt on the Split-End Post Route and we want to get one half player back to the opposite side of the field, we make a Cover 8 call. Now we are going to be playing Read Support with the safety to the Split-End side, and Cloud Support to the tight-end side with the corner. With this scheme we have the ability to play four different coverages and the kids only have to learn two different techniques. Also, we do have the ability to play Cover 3, and Man Coverages, and some Special Coverages. However, our bread and butter comes from Cover 2, 4, 6, and 8. We are going to play Cover 2 or 4 or some combinations of those two about 75 percent of the time.

Let me talk about Cover 2 and the basic responsibilities. We like to think of Cover 2 as a progression defense. In this order, in my opinion, is the way we want the defense to play. Collision, disruption, and making the receivers vary off their routes are the most important tasks on Cover 2. You have three weak spots in Cover 2. Everyone knows this. You have the Deep Middle and the two Fade areas. The way we try to stop that is by running a collision with the number 1, 2 strongside receivers, and the number 1 weakside receiver.

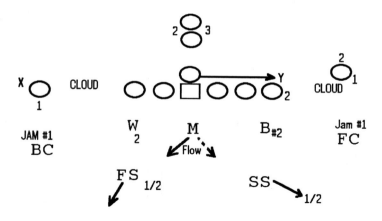

The field corner is going to be a Jam player to the Field. He is going to play Curl-Flat to the Field. The two safeties are going to be one half players. The boundary corner is going to be a Curl-Flat player. Our linebackers are what we call progression players. All five underneath players are progression players. We count the receivers from the outside to inside to the middle of the ball. If I am the field corner my progression is on the 1 man or Z Back. If I am the Buck backer my progression is on the 2 man or the Y End. The Mike backer is a Flow player. He will open to where the 3 man goes. The Will backer will open to where 2 Weak goes. The boundary corner is on the 1 Weak or X End.

We do cheat a little on this defense. If we are playing against an I-formation team, we use the term "Flow—Flow—Flow." We put a Flow Rule in for those teams, which I will cover later. What this tells us is this. If we get any full-flow action to the tight-end side, the boundary corner and the Will backer are going to use a Man Technique, or trowel position. If I am the boundary corner and we have communicated this before the snap of the ball; "Flow Rule—Flow Rule." If we get full flow away, we are going to get to a collision course on 1. If he is running a route and the boundary corner gets into position, he is going to get into a Man Underneath position on him with one half player behind him.

On that same action, if the Will backer gets full flow away, he is going to play the cutback run. After he plays the cutback run his eyes go across the field. He is going to fan the field and look for the next receiver coming back to him. On any receiver coming to him from the opposite side of the field, he is going to play a Man Technique on him. That is his base rule in the Read Technique. We end up playing Man on the back side and playing zone on the front side. Where does this help you? It allows you to be a little more aggressive with the linebackers by letting them play the run first and then react to the pass. Again, you have to play with what your personnel can do. We are blessed at Ohio State. We have three corners who can play coverage. That is base Cover 2.

What do you do with Mike and Buck on the I-back situation? Play-Action Passes have always been a problem for Cover 2. At one time we used the "Me-You" principle on the I-Backs Flow Rules. All the Me-You meant was that we were going to find out where the 2 receiver was. You always have a problem on this. If you get the Sprint Draw Action where the Fullback goes to the flat, it has not been a problem for us as far as getting the vertical. The Mike backer should be stacking for midaction and power plays. His eyes should be outside looking for the tight end. Our Buck backer should be stepping up to see the tight end, and we should get a good shot on him to begin with.

I mentioned that we play progression. If the fullback comes outside to the flat, and the tight end goes inside, we are going to our progression rule. In order to play our Cover 2 you must be able to count to 3. If you can get to 3 you are in good shape. As we step, our eyes go to our next progression. That is what we tell the linebackers. For example, if I am the Buck backer, and the tight end would release outside, as I open my eyes, I should go out to the next progression.

If my back goes flat, the Mike backer should check run and his eyes should go out to the next most dangerous progression. The Will backer should step, check, eyes go to the next most dangerous progression. That is what we are talking about in progression. Once your first key goes away, your eyes should pick up the next most dangerous progression. If everything continues to get wide, you continue to get width with them.

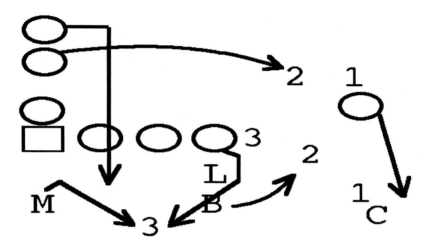

Question: What do we do against the backside slant route by X? That is our Flow rule. Both backs went Strong. Once the boundary corner reads flow, he should progress to his next key. We are going to jam the X End or 1 on the back side. As we jam him we are going to roll and get to his inside hip and play a Man Technique on him. That should be at the 6- to 7-yard area.

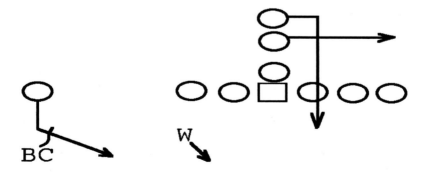

If he makes his slant early we should close hard on him because we have help behind us. On the same action, if the Will backer sees the same action, he should be closing. If nothing crosses his path he is going to continue to get depth. He should end up 6 to 7 yards deep straight off the ball. He is going to read the quarterback's eyes.

On Cover 4 it is the Read Principle to both sides. It is the same deal. We are working in triangles. The strong safety, Buck, and strong corner are getting a Read Call. Our free safety, Willie, and boundary corner are getting a Read Call. When we talk read we are talking about the safeties sitting down. If our presnap look is Cover 2, our safeties are going to be aligned somewhere between 11 and 12 yards deep, and 8 to 9 yards deep with our corners. On the snap of the ball the safeties *should not backpedal*. On any type of run action they should step down. Then they should get to a flat-foot read. Our corners will play a Man Technique on any vertical route at any depth we may want to establish. We put the term 10 yards on it. If it is a 10-yard vertical route, we cover them in Man.

If it is anything that goes across the field, they let it go and the read linebackers will pick it up. The safeties are going to sit. Both the Will backer and free safety on the Split-End side will read 2 weak. The strong safety, and in our situation, the Buck backer on the strong side, will read 2 strong.

They have three basic reads. The corners are man-to-man. If 2 goes to the Flat, we tell the Buck backer to jump him and play a Man Technique. One of the reasons we play a 9 Technique with the Leo is to make the tight end release inside. As the Buck sets, he sets his eyes outside on the tight end. He jumps the end man-to-man.

The field corner is going to sit in a flat-foot read. He ends up playing a Robber Technique. We want him to rob the Curl from 1 to that side, to the Dig to 1 to that side, and if they happen to run the Post, he will be underneath the route. If they run the Post it is the field corner's responsibility to stop the play. I am talking about the Deep Post, not necessarily the Slant.

The second read you will get from the strong safety and Buck position will be a vertical release where the tight end is coming up the field. It is the same situation. When we have a Read Call the collision and jam are not that important to us. We know that we have someone behind us. We have someone in the vertical area. If we get a vertical release coming off the ball, the strong safety is going to cushion and play outside in Man Technique on 2. When that happens, the Buck backer is going to Jam, and then he is going to end up being the Flat-Curl player. As he jams the tight end, he is going to open and look for 1. It is a tough situation if they are running the curl. As Buck comes outside he is looking for anything that crosses his face. He is looking for a back to flare out of the backfield, or a back-side shallow route, coming from another route. He will jump anything in his area. If nothing shows, he is going to hang in the Curl area.

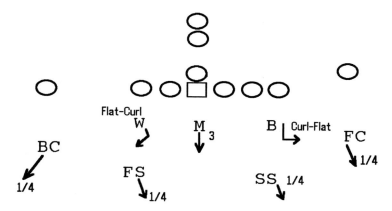

The Mike backer will open to the flow. All he is going to do is to play the Middle Hook to the Curl player to his side of flow. He is going to play the 3 receiver.

The third read is when the tight end goes shallow away from the wideout. The responsibility for the strong safety is going to be the same. He will normally check for a vertical receiver when he gets flow away. He will step to his key. He does not know initially if the receiver is going vertically or not. As the receiver goes away from him he is going to flat-foot it and try to get a read on the eyes of the quarterback. He now has the Rob on both sides. He has Curl from the front side to the Dig on the back side.

Let me show you a Split-Back Set. If we get this type of action, the Mike and Buck backers have a Me-You Call. We are talking about the linebackers now.

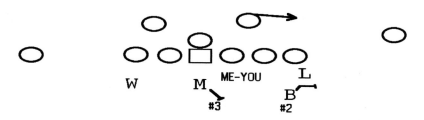

On Cover 2 Cloud the two linebackers are going to protect the middle of the field against the 2 receiver. Both linebackers are keyed into the 3 receivers as far as the run responsibilities are concerned. Will is keyed into 2 weak. If 3 steps outside, the Buck backer steps and looks for the tight end. He should think about an outside-in collision. The Mike backer should check, then his eyes go outside to his next progression. He should be thinking about the inside release by the tight end. When they start to separate, the progression changes. The Buck goes to the 2 man or the back going outside. The Mike backer should annihilate the tight end on any type of vertical release. If the end crosses, we are going to let him go and he will be picked up by the zone coverage.

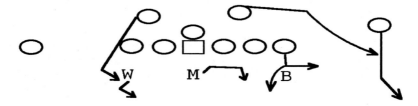

We have two basic rules for linebackers who are responsible for vertical routes. First, we want to get a jam on a receiver. That means to reroute him at least one step out of his route. If he gets by us on the vertical, we want the linebacker to get on his inside and run with him like a Man Technique. The Will backer has the same keys. If they go to the Flat he will hang in the Curl area. If 2 runs a vertical on him, he has the same responsibilities. We never want to let 2 or 3 get vertical on us. Once the offense goes to Split Backs we go to progression pass coverage.

Let's talk about Bootleg action and how we cover it. We are playing Cover 2 and we see the Bootleg. If we get strong flow we will step to the flow. We have an automatic term that we use. Once the backers recognize the Boot Action, the backer to the side the quarterback comes out to will sprint to the flat. After he gets there he looks for the first receiver to get there. We should be in a shuffle mode. We are playing the run first. Once we read Boot we should get to a Flat Mode. If nothing shows, I can be a secondary contain man if needed.

The Mike is taught to play the run first. Once he reads Boot he turns over his backside shoulder and tries to get depth at 7 to 10 yards. He looks for the backside man coming across. He looks over his backside shoulder to find out where the man is coming from. As he comes across he wants to get underneath his hip and then turn back and pick up the quarterback.

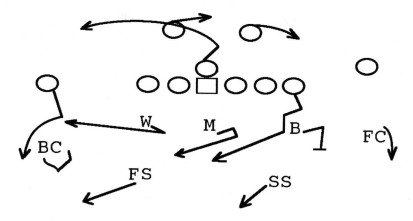

The man we have the most problems with is the backside crossing route. We should have the play covered with the Mike and Will backers playing the crossing action. That is against the Split Backs—Boot Weak.

If we have the Boot coming out of the I Set, the Will picks up 2 out of the backfield. That is part of his keys. He looks for the fullback coming out to the Flat.

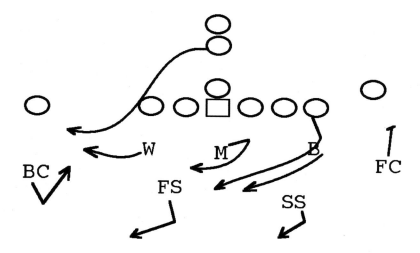

Again, if we get action away, the Will freezes. He can tell what the fullback is going to do by his angle. If he is going to cut off the defensive end, he will be coming up tight to the line of scrimmage. If he is pass releasing he will be a little flatter. That is easy to see as a linebacker. The Mike plays the play the same as he did before. That is how we cover the Boots on Cover 2.

On Cover 4 against the Boot it is different. It has helped us in Boot situations. Now we have our safeties involved. The linebackers do not change. They play with their same rules. We tell the safeties they are responsible for 2 on Play-Action Passes. The strong safety ends up as a middle free safety. The corners are man-to-man.

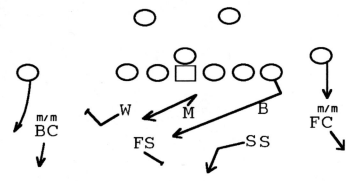

On Cover 4 against the I Set it is the same principle against the Weakside Boot. The Will backer jumps 2. The strong safety sits and flat reads. The corners play man-to-man on 1s. As the quarterback comes out, the free safety jumps and should be in position to split the zone. We tell the free safety to hold because he has 2 to his side on Play-Action Passes. But here we want him to hold at his depth at 8 to 10 yards and split the zone. The Mike does not change. We want the free safety in a Robber position on the crossing receiver. If the ball is passed to the flat he should be in position to break to the flat. The strong safety sinks to the middle and the field corner plays man on the back side.

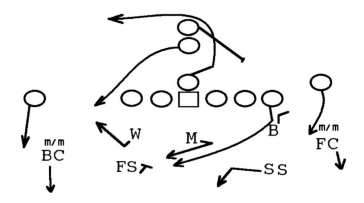

Let's talk the Flow Rule for Cover 2. We want our linebackers and secondary communicating before the snap of the ball. They should be calling "Read" or "Cloud" depending on the call we have on. The I Backs are set up. "Flow Rule—Flow Rule." All seven of our coverage players should know what is going on. Flow Rule tells us if we get Flow to the tight-end side, the boundary corner is going to play the Chase Position and play the backside one half. The free safety is playing one half. The Will backer is going to play his Read Technique. He looks for cutback plays; run first. Anything coming back to him he will pick up. If nothing comes to him he goes to a pure zone. Normally something will come to him on this action.

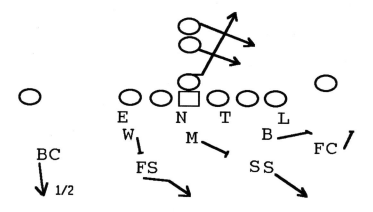

On the front side or the tight-end side of the play we are playing pure Cover 2 Zone. When we play Cover 4, the same principles are in effect. The two people affected when we play Cover 4 are the Will backer and the boundary corner.

Chapter 11

PASS COVERAGE IN THE EIGHT-MAN FRONT

Nick Saban
Michigan State University
1997

I want to talk about the eight-man front and man-to-man coverage. Most pro teams are playing this coverage now. More and more colleges are going to it, and you could play it very effectively in high school.

My view of the off-season program is what we need to develop in the players. I want to teach them how to give effort and develop mental toughness. We make it hard. We make them finish every play and give maximum effort. I see all those things as tremendous benefits. But if we don't sell that to the players, all they think is, "I'm tired of running every day." If that is their attitude about running, they are not going to do a very good job of it, because they are not goal oriented in their approach at all. They don't see the light at the end of the tunnel. We didn't make a very good road map for them so they could understand why they were doing what they were doing and how it was going to benefit them.

I feel we have done a much better job with our team because of our understanding. Does that mean we are compromising our values, principles, and integrity with the way we go about coaching? Not at all. But we can do our job better when we understand where they are coming from. Believe me when I tell you that.

I think the reason we exist as coaches is to help people be successful. If they are successful, we will win games. How do you get them to be successful? The key is consistency in performance. That makes anyone successful in whatever they do. Success is based on performance. What makes people have good performance? They have to want to do it. That is the most important thing.

As coaches, our perception is that these things are good for you. We are establishing discipline, learning how to give effort, and learning how to finish plays. But to the players, it is a pain in the butt, and it is hard. Therefore, they have no goals or direction. How could they like it, do well at it, and be committed to it? They have no reason to be committed to it, because we didn't sell it to them correctly.

Highly motivated people give consistency in performance. Motivation comes from knowing what you want accomplished and being committed to it. Even if you know what you want to accomplish, what does it take to do it? Your attitude is made up of your habitual thoughts, habits, and priorities on a day-to-day basis. You can have good or bad thoughts, habits, or priorities, but you control those things. We can change those. If they are bad, we can make them good. That is where it all starts.

Sometimes young people need direction. It all starts with your attitude. The sum of all those habits, thoughts, and priorities is your character. That tells what kind of person you really are. That takes into account the decision you make when the coach is not watching. It takes a lot of character and self-discipline to be committed to something that you want to accomplish. It takes a lot to see it through to the finish.

The first thing is to work and invest your time in something that is important to you. That is critical to being successful in anything. Don James used to say, "You reap what you sow." He was my college coach. He talked about two farmers. One guy worked from sunup to sundown. The other guy sat on his porch all day. When harvest came, the guy who worked hard had the biggest harvest you could possibly have. The guy who sat on his porch had nothing. The price you pay for success must be paid in advance. There is no way you can be successful and not pay the price up front and in advance. It never just happens. You have to make a tremendous investment in it. Invest your time in something. Don't spend it.

The second thing is that you have to stick with it. You have to be persistent and learn from your mistakes. It is so difficult to coach guys right now. They are so self-centered and selfish. So are my kids. It is the way young people are today. It doesn't make any difference how old they are. They have too many choices. They never have to make any commitments to anything. If they are not making any baskets today, they go over and hit golf balls. If the range is a little hot, they go swim in the pool at the country club. If the water is too cold, they go play baseball. They swing three times and miss, so they go do something else. That's what my kids do.

When I grew up in West Virginia in a coal-mining town, we had a company store, and that was it. We had a ball diamond. The company owned it all. When you got up to bat, there was nothing else to do. You kept swinging until you hit it. Most of us hit it pretty good because we didn't have a choice. We made a commitment to doing it because there was nothing else to do. It is not that way now.

As coaches, we always tell our players what they did wrong, but we seldom ever tell them what they did right. I think you have to find ways to reinforce positive performance in the way you coach. You need to be more positive with the players. They always respond better that way.

They have to learn that there is a seed for every good thing in every mistake they make. There is a learning experience in those mistakes. Old Buck Nystrom used to beat our guys with a stick. But they responded to it, and he was one of the better coaches I've ever been around. They used to say to him, "Coach me, coach." That is what he tried to convince them of. They wanted to learn, so he got to them. They took it and respected him. That is what you need to have.

They have to be positive about the negative mistakes they have. They have to see that they are learning from that and growing. In doing that, they learn how to overcome adversity as well.

Our team right now, to me, is right at the choke phase. We are right where we can choke when it counts. That is not negative. I think you have to be damn good to choke. You can't be in a 29–29 game in the fourth quarter with Penn State and not be very good. You can't get ahead of Iowa 23–10 going into the fourth quarter and not be very good. But when it got thick in the end, we had too many young players. We didn't have enough prime-time warriors who believed they could make the big play at the end of a game. When they started having that little bit of doubt, they took the apple. They made mistakes they had never made before.

We got a turnover against Penn State on the 14 with less than four minutes to go in the game. We followed that with the three worst plays we had run in the football game. We had 550 yards and got three straight plays with negative yards. After that, we missed the field goal. The guy hadn't missed a field goal inside the 30-yard line all year.

Next, the defense came on the field. We had second and long. We doubled the slot receiver. He ran straight across the field. We were playing him inside and outside. The guy who was supposed to take him inside just looked at him. He caught the pass and ran 36 yards into field-goal position for them with less than two minutes to go. We had played the coverage three or four times before correctly. What happened to that guy? I'm not blaming the kid. I'm saying we are not at a level of maturity where guys believe that they can make the play.

In the Michigan game, we were behind 14–10. We went into our two-minute offense with 50 seconds left in the first half. We were on the 50-yard line. We threw an interception, and the guy returned it to our 10-yard line. They scored with 19 seconds left on the clock. They kicked off, and we fumbled the kickoff. They went right in and scored again. With 15 seconds left in the half, they scored 14 points. The second half and the rest of the game, we played all right. Can you overcome that adversity? It is difficult against good football teams. All the teams that I was talking about are good football teams.

I think that all these things come from not believing in yourself, having self-imposed limitations on yourself as to what you can and can't accomplish. They don't have enough confidence in themselves that they can make the play in the most critical time of the game to win the game. That comes from mental toughness and a lot of self-confidence.

Self-imposed limitations are the doubt we all have. How many times have you as a coach been sitting in the locker room before a big game and had doubts about whether you can win or not? It happens to me sometimes. It happens to your players, too.

There was the fisherman in West Virginia. He went fishing. He caught a big fish and a little fish. He threw the big fish back in and kept the little fish. I asked him why he didn't keep the big fish and throw the little one back. He said that he only had a nine-inch frying pan. He put limitations on himself as to what kind of fisherman he could be by what kind of frying pan he had.

I ask our players sometimes how big a frying pan they have. How much confidence do they have? It is important to develop an attitude that you can be successful with.

I can't speak at a clinic without talking about this stuff. I think that's the essence of getting intangibles out of football players. They are simple things like giving effort, playing with toughness, being responsible for your own self-determination, and knowing what you are supposed to do. Those things sound really simple, but how many games do we lose on mental mistakes? How many times do you watch a film where someone is not loafing? How many times do you see your team not demonstrate the kind of toughness, physically and mentally, that you would like for them to play with? Those are all intangibles. It takes no ability to do these things, but very few times do we see them. You have to have a well-conditioned team to be able to do it. If you are not a well-conditioned team, that is when you make mistakes. They make mental mistakes, loaf, and lack toughness when they are tired. Who said, "Fatigue makes cowards of us all"? Of course, you know that it was Vince Lombardi.

Let's talk about Cover 1. The term MOF means middle-of-the-field safety. Anything that has this type of coverage is taught with the same principles and theory. Whether we play three-deep zone with strong rotation or three-deep zone with weak rotation, the principles of every position remain the same. Whether we teach man-free Cover 1 with the safety down strong or man-free Cover 9 with the safety down weak, the principles stay the same. The whole concept of this coverage depends on the area played by the free safety. We feel that a free safety can cover about 35 yards deep and 5 yards outside either hash mark when he is in the middle of the field. For everybody on the defensive field to use the safety's help, he must reroute, funnel, and play leverage on receivers relative to the middle-of-the-field safety.

This coverage starts with the corners. The college football field is a little different from the high school field. The hash marks are 19 yards from the sideline and 13½ yards apart. The yard-line numbers are 7 yards to the bottom and 9 yards to the top from the sideline.

Ten yards from the sideline with the ball in the middle of the field is what I call a divider for the corner. If the receiver is inside the divider of the corner, the corner plays an outside alignment. That is because the safety is in the middle of the field and is relatively close for the post cut of the receiver. If the receiver aligns outside the corner's divider, the corner aligns inside, because the relative distance to the safety where he helps the corner has increased.

The divider determines whether the corner plays inside or outside the receiver. We tell him to play inside or outside relative to the divider. The divider is a plane that runs all the way down the field. If the receiver lines up inside the divider but stems the corner to a position outside the divider, the corner goes from an outside position on the receiver to an inside one.

We tell our safety that if the ball is thrown 25 yards, he should be able to break that far. We teach a little different theory with zone and man coverage.

In three-deep zone, the free safety has to stay as deep as the deeper receiver. When we play man, we settle the free safety at 25 yards. We feel that the one thing that can hurt us is running the post and the dig. If they throw to the dig receiver, there can be no one there unless the corner plays a perfect coverage. The safety needs to jump everything in the middle of the field.

Here is the second concept I want to show you. In a three-deep zone or a middle-of-the-field safety coverage, there are areas on the field that you don't want people to run in. Those areas are the seams of the zone. For the high school field, the seam is 17 yards from the sideline and 3 yards wide. The seam starts at 14 yards from the sideline and ends at 17 yards from the sideline. If you let receivers run down those seams, the safety can't cover those areas. You have to keep people out of those areas if you are playing middle-of-the-field coverage.

When we play a three-deep zone, someone always drops to the seam and reroutes the receivers out of the seams at 10 yards. If we reroute the receiver at 5 yards, he can run past the defender and get back into the seam. If we reroute him at 10 yards, it is late in the play, and he doesn't have enough time to get back on the seam before he is too deep.

The same thing is true of Cover 2. We reroute receivers at 10 yards out or in to the seam. The seam in a Cover 2 is the half-defender divider. That creates a leverage field position for the half-field safety.

With the three-deep zone, we want the receivers out of the seams, and with two-deep, we want them in the seams.

Let me show you our Cover 1. I'll draw this up as an eight-man front. The corners in our defense would be in bump-and-run man on the two wide receivers. The strong safety and three linebackers are responsible for the backs and tight end. The free safety plays over the top in this coverage. The Will linebacker has the split-end side break, and the strong safety has the tight-end side break. Break means "if the formation splits someone else out." If the tailback aligns in the slot to the split-end side, the Will linebacker is responsible for him. That is only for the backs. The corners have the wide receivers all the time.

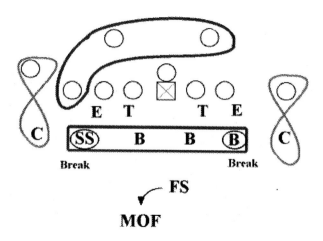

If the offense brings both wide receivers to the same side, we bring both of our corners over to that side. You may do it differently, but whoever starts out on the tight end has tight-end side breaks, and the Will linebacker always has split-end side breaks. That means we will never have a Will linebacker cover a wide receiver. These two formations are the only ones they can make with normal personnel in the game.

If one of the backs goes in motion to the split end, the Will linebacker covers him. If one of them goes in motion to the tight-end side, the strong safety has him.

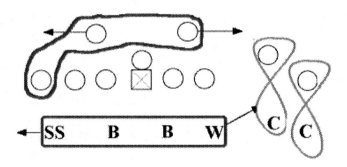

Let me get into the techniques of coverage. The divider for the corner is 1 yard on top of the numbers, or 10 yards from the sideline. If I teach a corner to play bump and run, the first thing I want to do is make sure he understands the divider principle. If the receiver is inside the divider, the corner is aligned outside and on his low shoulder. If the receiver is outside the divider, the corner aligns inside and plays high-shoulder position. The receiver wants to get on top because he can go anywhere he wants from that position. We take that away from him. We get on top and cut him off. If the receiver is inside the divider, the corner will be outside and on the low shoulder. If the receiver runs a flag route outside the divider, the corner can easily get to the high shoulder and cut him off.

In the bump-and-run, the corner should off-hand jam the receiver. If the receiver aligns right on the divider, the corner aligns outside and low. The corner watches the hips of the receiver. As long as the hips are square, the corner is square. As soon as he starts to turn his hips one way or the other, the corners off-hand jams him. If the break is to the inside, the corner jams with his outside hand. If the break is outside, the corner jams with his inside hand. We try to hit between the receiver's shoulder tips and near tip.

Bump-and-run is the best coverage you can play against anybody, even with marginal athletes. You have a better chance playing guys up on receivers than you do off. The hardest thing to do in man coverage is to play off a receiver and cover him. It is the hardest thing to teach. The corner has to have great feet, be able to redirect, and have a great burst to the ball. Plus, the receiver knows whether he is going, and you don't. When you get up and bump, you are in position to cover the guy, as long as you stay in position and get your hands on the receiver.

Most guys make the mistake of widening their feet and setting back when the receiver breaks. As soon as a defensive back gets in that position, he is beat. To get out of that position, the defensive back has to step back inside his frame to be able to go anywhere. What the back wants to do is keep his feet together, so that when the receiver starts his move, the back can slide into him, jam him, and be on top of him. That is the most important thing in bump coverage.

To keep the receiver from walking all over the defensive back, we use a punch at the line to force a release. Just as soon as the receiver moves, the defensive back punches him with the inside hand on the inside tip of the receiver. When that happens the receiver's coach is going to tell him to lean back.

The other thing you can do is to fake a punch. The receiver leans back, and that slows his release. If the defensive back reaches with the wrong hand in bump and run, he is dead. The most natural thing for the defensive back to do is throw both hands up and squat. Either one of those things kills you in bump and run.

We want to protect the middle of the field in bump-and-run. We give up the out route. Make them throw the ball in the flat, but don't let them throw the ball over your head outside. Those are the hardest passes to complete, so everything is relative to that.

If the receiver takes an inside break, the defensive back jams him the same way. That puts him inside the divide line. The defensive back assumes the low-shoulder position and rides him down the field. If the receiver cuts outside, he is cutting into the defender. If he breaks inside, the defender works down on him, always dragging his back hand so he can hook the receiver. That is the technique in a nutshell.

I could give you a list of drills to do to practice this. You can step and mirror the receiver on release using no hands. Step and slide on the release using no hands. You can do the same drills using the off hands. You have to teach kids to roll over quickly. Kids who play all their life in the off position have trouble turning. If they are turned left and they have to go right, they always slow-turn. When you play close coverage, if you slow-turn, you're dead. When the receiver disappears behind the defensive back, the defender has to speed-turn into him. That is the drill we teach. The receiver runs down the field, making the defender roll-turn. Everything you do in close coverage is done with the speed turn.

Everson Walls ran about 4.9 in the 40. He could not backpedal a step. He could not run a lick, but he always had his man cut off. He always used his help and had 39-inch arms to jam the hell out of people. He was a very effective player and never played in a backpedal. He could half-turn with the best of them, which meant he always had the receiver cut off.

Let's go to the strong safety on the tight end. The first thing we want to know is the alignment of the tight end inside or outside the divider. Most tight ends will be inside the divider. We play our strong safety like a rover back. He aligns 3 yards outside the tight end and 5 yards deep. If the tight end releases upfield, the strong safety runs to his outside shoulder and gets in a low position. He wants to get on the tight end as soon as he can. We never want to play a tight end or a big man in a high position, because he will push off the defender and come back for the ball.

The tight end releases to the outside, and the strong safety plays him on the divider. If the tight end runs into the seam, the strong safety should play even with him. If the safety plays low-shoulder, the quarterback can shoot the ball in there. If the safety plays high-shoulder and the quarterback throws at the back pad, he's got the safety too. We run shoulder to shoulder in the seam. Ideally, we want to run the tight end out of the seam. When the tight end runs to the seam, the safety beats him there and makes him break one way or the other. When he breaks, the safety rolls into him and plays his technique.

Let's talk about the three linebackers and the strong safety playing the backs and the tight end. When you are playing middle-of-the-field coverage in man to man, you should never play in-and-out coverage

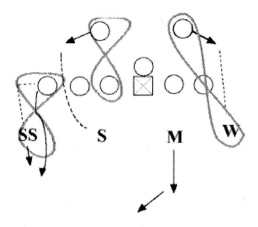

with the tight end and near back. If the tight end runs up the field, the strong safety takes him. If the backs split and go different directions, the Sam linebacker takes the left back coming out, and the Will linebacker takes the right back coming out. The Mike linebacker backs up in the middle of the field to cut any player who comes in the middle of the field. If no one comes into the middle 5 to 7 yards deep, he continues to back up to help on the dig route.

The Mike linebacker always has the second back out to a side. If both backs flow strong or weak, the Mike linebacker has the second back. If both backs flow weak, the Will linebacker has the first back. The Mike linebacker has the second back. The Sam linebacker becomes what I call the rat. That comes from a rat in a hole. He is the middle player, waiting to cut anything that comes into the middle. The strong safety has the tight end. If the tight end runs a drag across the field, he runs into the rat, who picks him up. The strong safety becomes the rat. That gives us a free guy in the hole both short and deep. We are playing 4 on 3 with all the receivers leveraged off.

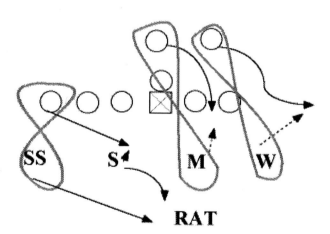

If the offense runs a flow or play-action pass to the strong side, the Sam linebacker has the first back out of the backfield. The Mike linebacker has the second back. The strong safety has the tight end. The Will linebacker is the rat. If the tight end runs the drag, the Will linebacker cuts him. The strong safety becomes the rat and could get under the dig route of the split end.

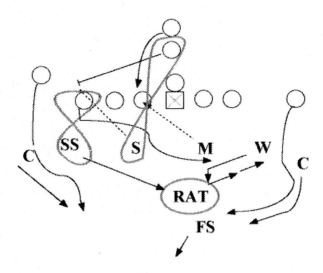

Whoever the free guy is out of the four becomes the rat and cuts off the receivers. The only time the safety gets cut is when the tight end goes across. If the tight end goes vertical, the safety plays outside and the low shoulder. The safety in the sky-force position never has to cover the tight end on an inside move.

Because you are playing 4 on 3, no one is in a run-pass conflict. Everyone can play their gap responsibility on a run and still play pass responsibility without a problem.

Here is a way to work things into your package. Anytime that the safety takes the tight end and the tight-end-side breaks, we call that Cover 1. We could call 0, which means five guys rushing with no rat in the hole.

If we call Cover 9, the Will linebacker would have the tight end, and the safety would come down weak. It is all the same principle of coverage. What we don't want to happen is to have a linebacker covering a speedster out of the backfield. The strong safety aligns to the split end and has split-end-side breaks. The free safety is in the middle deep but has tight-end-side breaks. That gives us a safety playing that speedster out of the backfield instead of a linebacker. If the free safety takes a tight-end-side break, the strong safety rotates to the middle and becomes the middle-of-the-field safety. The three linebackers play the remaining back and the tight end. That leaves us a rat short in the middle.

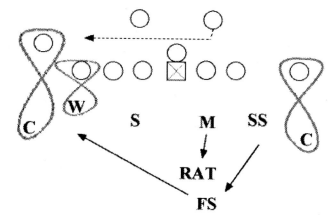

The hardest pattern to cover is the double cross by the tight end and slot back. The first thing you do when you get cut off from the receiver who you are covering is to look through the guy who cut you to see whether anything is coming. If there is, it is an automatic cut to the other guy back. That is the first thing. Guys won't do that sometimes. As soon as they get cut off their man, they want to fade back into the hole. What this ends up looking like is a soft zone about 5 to 7 yards deep. When the linebacker gets the cut call, he looks through the guy who cut him and picks up the pattern coming the other way. That way, they don't have to change directions but once.

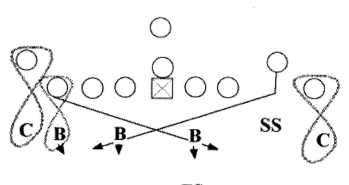

This coverage will play well in nickel coverage. It plays an eight-man front in the nickel. It will play against four wideouts. It will play against three wideouts and a tight end. In every situation, it makes a front with one more man than the offense has. If you play against four wideouts, you have six in the box and can play the coverage. If they have a tight end, three wideouts, and one back in the game, you have seven guys in the box, and the offense has six to block you. All you need is two guys to play corner. That is why the corners in the NFL always make more money than safeties.

We teach all our coverages the same way. If we play zone, we play Cover 3 and 6. When we teach three-deep zone, we teach relationships. We have a flat player who relates to number 1. We have a hook player who relates to number 2 weak. We have a hook player strong who relates to number 3. We have a flat player strong who relates to number 2. We have a corner–corner–free safety in the three-deep coverage. Our weak-side rotation is Cover 6. Our strong-side rotation is Cover 3. We teach the drops to everyone.

The progression in zone for us is to drop, reroute a receiver, match the pattern after the pattern distribution, and break on the ball. Matching the pattern after the pattern distribution is another talk. We number the receivers from the outside in on both sides. The flanker strong would be 1, tight end 2, and the back to that side would be 3. The split end weak would be l, and the running back to that side would be 2. The flanker does a curl, the tight end hooks, and the strong back runs a flat. After the pattern distribution, the back is 1, flanker 2, and tight end 3. This coverage is like man to man, except you don't have a man. If a receiver comes into your zone, he is your man. That is pattern matching. This is good because you don't get picked off.

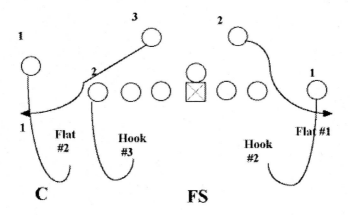

Chapter 12

DEFENDING TODAY'S PASSING GAME

Jerry Sandusky
Penn State University
1993

I have been asked to talk on Defending Today's Passing Game. Obviously, it is becoming more difficult to defend the pass. It is true because of the types of offenses people are using. The main reason is because of the liberalized blocking rules used today. The great skilled athletes playing the game today have a big impact on the game. Today there is a great amount of emphasis placed on the passing game. It isn't as much fun to defend the offenses today as it once was. It is more of a challenge to defend the passing game today.

Before you consider putting together a defensive package to defend today's passing game, there are some personnel considerations that are very important. I could stand up here and draw pass coverage after pass coverage to use against the passing game. However, at our level the first priority comes down to pass rush. You are not going to be able to play in our league, or any level, if you do not have the ability to apply pressure on the quarterback with your front four people. You may have to blitz and do other things on defense to get pressure on the quarterback. If you can't, you will have problems. You had better have some players that can rush the passer when you consider personnel on defense. You must have quickness on the corner. If you are going to sack the quarterback you must have the ability to get to him with one of your outside rushers. We talk about speed and quickness on the outside and power and explosion on the inside. We feel you need at least one outstanding Cover Corner on defense. We feel we can get by with one person that can go outside and hold his own against the pass. If you can eliminate that part of the field and concentrate on the inside, it will make your job a lot easier. With the use of the one-back set used today, it is more important that we have inside linebackers that are more capable of moving. It is more and more important if you are going to play man-to-man because you get matched up with outstanding skilled players.

Our defensive scheme is a mobile one. It involves multiple fronts and multiple coverages. I will quickly go over the type of personnel we use at each position. If we had to say what our defense is we would say we are in a stack arrangement. This past year we flip-flopped everyone. Our Willie and tackle always go to the tight-end side. The nose and end are our other two down linemen, and they go away from the tight end. They are our front four rushers. We start out in a Two-Deep Alignment. We have a strong corner to the open field, and a weak corner into the boundary. We flip-flop our linebackers. The Sam linebacker goes to the strong side, the backer linebacker goes to the strong side, and the Fritz goes to the weak side. Our Hero is our strong safety. Our other safety is our Free Safety.

BASE DEFENSE

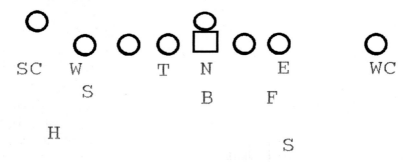

Let me run down the characteristics of the people we look for in filling those positions. Our most mobile big people have to be playing defense. They must be able to move. That does not mean they have to run 4.8, but they do have to have outstanding quickness.

The nose is a more compact player. He must be able to defend against the run. It is hard to get much pass rush out of that position because he is getting blocked from all angles. The tackle is a better pass rusher. He is larger and more explosive. The end plays with his hand down. He does not stand up. He aligns on the outside leg of the tackle in our base defense. He has to be mobile enough to be a good pass rusher.

He has to be able to play the quarterback on the option. He must be able to contain on sprint-out passes. He is a linebacker-type player.

Our stand-up players are our linebackers. Willie is our stand-up linebacker on the tight end. He is our strongest linebacker. He is in a two-point stance. We will move him around. He must have the same qualities as the end. He must be an outstanding pass rusher. Our Sam linebacker is the most athletic of the linebackers. He aligns to the open field. He is a combination of an outside linebacker and a strong safety. He will play on the line of scrimmage and in the backfield. He is an outstanding athlete. He will have to move outside as a strong safety versus Twins. He will get isolated on the second receiver versus Trips and have to play man-to-man at times. He is an exceptional football player for us.

Fritz is the second most active linebacker. He aligns into the boundary. He is a combination linebacker. He will shift and move inside and play inside linebacker at times.

The Backer linebacker is a quarterback type. He is the leader. He is a good athlete. He does not have to have the coverage skills that the Sam and Fritz linebackers have. He may have to cover the number 3 receiver versus Trips if we are in man-to-man. We would never do that unless he had help behind him.

Our strong corner is our best coverage player. He must be able to go outside and hold his own against a wide receiver. He must be an excellent athlete with outstanding speed. The weak corner is also a good coverage player. He is more involved in run support.

The Hero is a combination underneath player and a deep defender. He must have good judgment. He must be a good run-support player. He lines up on the strong side. He is in on more run support than the Strong Corner.

Our free safety is our center fielder. He is our leader in the secondary. He is the person with good judgment. He is the game saver with his tackle.

The next area I want to discuss relates to our pass rush. I am not going to stand up here and demonstrate the pass-rush techniques, but I am going to give you some of the impressions that I have had through the years. I believe pass rush is a very innate thing. I do not think you can necessarily coach good pass rushers. They have to have great quickness and explosion, and they must have a sense of timing about them. Here are some general observations I consider important:

- You must get a good jump on the football.
- You have to be a smart football player.
- You have to anticipate.
- You must have a good stance.
- You must study the other team's stances and figure out who is going to block you on the pass rush.
- You must know the situation.

We attack with our front four in general. They are going to be moving forward at all times. We are going to read on the run. We have been doing that for years. This should help us even if we do not anticipate a passing situation.

We want to get a wide corner or a wide rusher if possible. We want to attack. We want to be offensive. We want to force the blocker to move laterally to protect his outside, or he is going to get run over. We want to establish two basic pass rushes. We have a Speed Rush on the outside and a Power Rush on the inside as a premise. We want to force the offensive tackle to move out laterally. We want to get him in an awkward body position. We want to establish the Power Rush, or Bull Rush, on the inside so the offensive lineman is a little concerned that he is going to get run over. If you can't establish this, you are going to have problems. If you do not have a threat inside and outside, they will block you without much problem. We call these moves the Bull Rush and Speed Rush.

We do not want to get hooked up with the offensive linemen. If you get hooked up with them you have all kinds of problems. They grab you and hold you and do whatever they can to keep you from getting to the passer. Get their hands off you. Don't get hooked up with them. Operate with the elbows inside.

We must have a sense of timing on the pass rush. We want to maintain the rush up the field. We must know when to push and when to pull by the blocker. We want to get our hands up when the quarterback is ready to throw the football. Again, that is a sense of timing. My boss is always yelling, "Get those hands up; get those hands up." This used to bother me when I first started coaching. I got sick of hearing him screaming about getting the hands up in the air. I studied the situation and now it doesn't bother me.

Let me give you some Pass-Rush Twist versus the Dropback Pass. A Twist is used in order to take advantage of pass protection schemes and to keep the offensive blocker off balance.

ON THE SNAP—Two defenders change lanes on the snap. It's more effective vs. man-to-man protection.

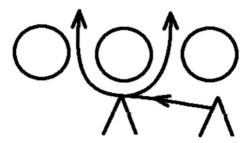

ON KEY—Two defenders exchange pass-rush lanes on key. (Use only against a drop-back pass.)

COMBINATION—One defender drives into a gap on the snap. The other defender reads to determine run or pass then exchanges lanes versus a drop-back pass.

In discussing Pass Coverage we certainly do not have all of the answers. I will share some thoughts with you. Two things that seems to be common in our thinking in putting together our pass coverage scheme is disruption of receivers and disguising the coverage. With that in mind we begin our teaching with a Two-Deep Zone.

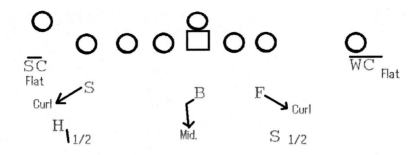

Both corners are responsible for the flat. They assume a press alignment slightly outside the wide receivers as close to the line of scrimmage as possible. Their feet are parallel and shoulders square to the
line of scrimmage. As a first priority, they try to jam the receivers
(disrupt his release). This is accomplished by sliding laterally and
stripping the receiver with their hands. They must not get overex-
tended or let the receiver have an easy outside release. We want to
disrupt or cause a very flat release in any direction. If the receiver
inside releases, the corner slides then opens to the inside and retreats laterally to a depth of about 12 yards depending on the situation. If necessary, the corner should be ready to sink to the outside
and be ready for a corner route. When the defender has gotten enough
depth, he should be ready to drive off his back foot and attack any
receiver that shows in front of him.

If the ball is thrown over the defender's head, he should turn his
shoulders and sprint at an angle to make the interception. If the receiver takes a flat outside release, the defender should slide and then
pivot back to the inside. Again, he retreats laterally and sinks outside
to protect the hole between him and the safety.

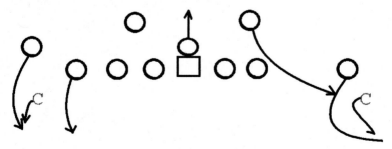

As far as the linebackers are concerned, this is how we play it. The
Sam and Fritz are responsible for the Curl Pass Zones. If the ball is in
the middle of the field, the curls are 1 yard inside the hash mark, 12

yards deep. When the ball is on the hash mark, the open field curl is 3 yards inside the hash and the boundary curl is 3 yards outside the hash mark.

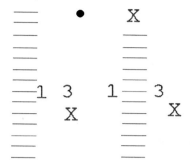

Before they go to the curl zone they must not let the number 2 receivers go straight down the field easily. They force these receivers wide to the curl zones.

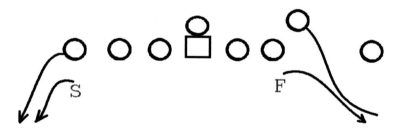

It is also significant to note that the only people who curl are the wide receivers. En route to the Curl, the defenders should run laterally and glance for the widest receiver. They should settle at the angle they have retreated, stopping approximately 3 yards in front of and to the inside of the receiver threatening the curl.

The Backer is responsible for the middle zone. The location of the middle zone is 15 yards deep in the middle of the field, 5 yards inside the hash mark if the ball is on the hash mark. The first threat to the middle zone is the number 2 receiver. Attention should be focused first on number 2, then number 3.

The Hero and safety align on the hashes and retreat straight down the hash mark reading the inside receivers. When they are sure there is not a deep middle threat, they can widen and play over top the wideout.

When we are playing Zone Coverage we want to hang back and react up to anything that is thrown in front of us. This makes us vulnerable to some double-level passes. The next thing in our teaching progression to help ourselves with this problem, we go to some type of Man Under. As a compliment to the Two-Deep Zone, we incorporate the Two-Deep Man Coverage.

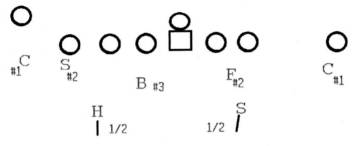

Trying to disguise the coverage as much as possible, the corners move to inside alignments on the wide receivers. Now the corners set and take away the inside release of the receiver. They try to join the receiver and must not overreact to any outside fakes. When the receiver has gotten beyond the defender's outside shoulder, he turns and runs with him, mirroring him from underneath. He should concentrate on the receiver, especially his hands. When his hands go up, the defender should bring his hands up through the receiver's hands and turn to look for the ball. The safety should shout "Ball."

The Sam and Fritz linebackers play the number 2 receivers in the same manner. The Backer is responsible for handling the number 3 receiver. If playing a receiver who is aligned in the backfield, the defender attacks the back through his inside half then mirrors him staying underneath to his inside.

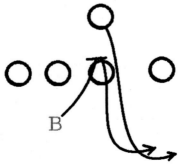

Disguising from a Two-Deep look, our next progression is to have the strong corner finesse out of his press alignment and we Roll Weak to Three Deep. We want to be in the best open-field front defense we can be in because of the option. We will not get great run support on the strong side.

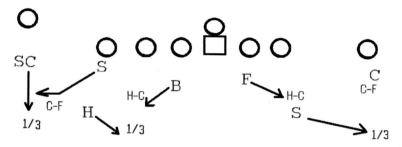

SC: Back out and play outside 1/3 zone.

H: Roll to deep middle 1/3 zone.

S: Roll to weak outside 1/3 zone.

WC: Play number 1 recklessly unless number 2 shows flat then play up to number 2.

F: Start to curl zone reading number 2. If number 2 goes flat, continue to curl. If number 2 comes straight down, latch on to him in the hook area. If number 2 blocks or goes strong, go to the middle.

B: Start to curl reading number 2. If 2 goes flat, continue to get width to the curl. If he comes straight down, he should latch on to him in the hook area. If number 2 blocks, hang in the middle.

S: Start for the wide curl. Top of the numbers in the middle of the field, hash mark if the ball is on the hash mark. Read number 2. Hang in the wide curl and play up to anything that shows flat.

Because of all of the bootleg plays we are seeing, we have gone to a Four-Deep Secondary to try to play better pass defense. Some of the teams that are playing the best pass defense are those that are getting eight people around the football. They pressure the heck out of the offense. In order to get to an eight-man front, the weak corner can move into an alignment 3 yards outside the nearest defender at a depth of 3 yards. The safety moves out to a position slightly outside the widest receiver on the wide side. The Hero moves close to his middle 1/3 zone. Obviously, the disguise is very limited. We are seeing teams that want to stretch us across the field. We want to be able to bring people on both sides. That is foremost in our thinking in bringing those people from both sides so we can blitz.

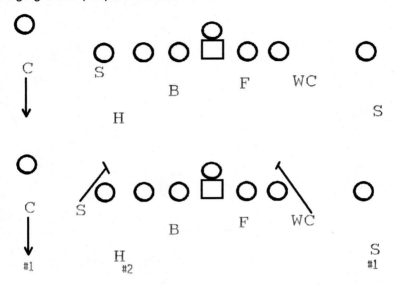

Having eight people around the ball provides the opportunity for quick perimeter pressure. By rushing both Sam and the weak corner, the coverage that is played is three-deep man-to-man.

In this coverage the strong corner and safety play more cautiously when covering the receiver. They start to backpedal then run laterally striving to maintain inside position keeping a cushion of 2 to 3 yards. The inside linebackers play the same as in Two-Deep Man.

In addition to the Roll Weak to Three Deep we rotate to a Strong Three-Deep. The Hero and strong corner can either roll or invert.

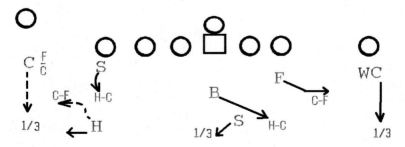

If a roll call is made, the corner presses and plays curl to flat while the Hero plays the outside 1/3. If an invert call is made, the Hero plays curl to flat and the strong corner has the outside 1/3. The Sam and Backer handle hook to curl. Fritz plays curl to flat. The safety has the middle third while the weak corner retreats and plays the outside 1/3.

As a change of pace in the underneath zones, we might flood the zones Strong or Weak. Strong flood coverage would have the Sam in the curl, Backer in the middle, and the Fritz playing curl to flat.

Weak flood coverage would have the Fritz in the weak flat, Backer in the weak curl, Sam in the middle, and Hero curl to flat.

Regardless of the defensive scheme it is very important to have a sound system. You do not want to do any more than is necessary. Success comes with good players, discipline, concentration, and aggressive play.

Next I want to talk about our drills to teach the defense. First, I will talk about pass-rush drills. We stress stance, start, and individual techniques.

BULL RUSH

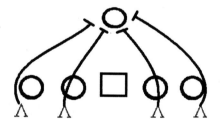

QUARTERBACK SCRAMBLE

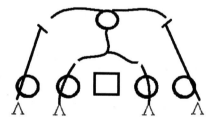

STRAIGHT DROP-BACK

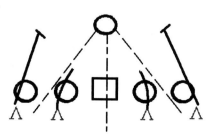

SPRINT AND SPRINT SCRAMBLE

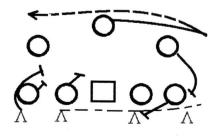

After we get through those drills we add two backs. Again, we are going to run a combination of drills. We will work on the Drop-back Throw, Drop-back Scramble, Sprint, and Sprint Scramble.

We use the same type of progression with our linebackers. We are going to put them in a terminal position. We want them to have a feel for the depth of the drop and to see where the quarterback and receivers are during a pass. We put him 19 yards deep and we have two dummies 3 yards behind him. The coach will simulate throwing the ball to force the linebacker to make his break. We want to see if the linebacker is turning the shoulders and sprinting. We want to see if he reacts properly. Once we get him moving properly, we throw the football. Now he catches the ball and sprints back to the coach.

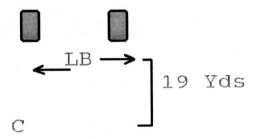

After we teach him to move on the ball, we want him to retreat to that terminal position. We want to give him a feel for the area he is to cover. From that point, he retreats to a receiver. Now the coach throws the football.

The next phase would be to take them as a unit and have them retreat to their pass zones. We work on the techniques of getting back to our zones. Later we will have them go back to their zones and we throw the ball and have them break full speed on the ball.

The next phase is to teach them to determine some pattern reaction and recognition. We want to break that down so they have an idea where the receivers are coming from. We work on all the different patterns they will see in a game.

We move to the secondary and use the same principles. We start the backs on their backpedal. We have them back up and we check their stance and their retreat. The next phase is to change directions. They have to react on the move. The coach will predetermine how they are going to turn. The next stage is to get them to react to what a receiver does. We do not tell them how to react. The next thing is to get the back on his backpedal and then have him come back up on the play. We are working on techniques. First, we predetermine the moves and then we have them react on the coach.

We do the simple Down-The-Line Drill so they learn to rotate their hips. They cross over and run laterally. They cross over back and forth as they go down the line. We are changing body position as we go down that line.

We do the Diamond Mirror Drill. We have four defensive backs in the drill with the coach. We have three of them on defense and one on offense. The coach tells the offensive player where to run with the ball. The other three backs must *mirror* the offensive back. After the offensive back goes once he replaces one of the three backs.

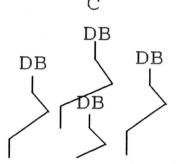

Some other things we have done through the years is to use our linebackers to make special underneath adjustments. If you do not have the capability to play man-to-man, you can use this. You may have a good pass rush but can't play man-to-man. You may want to consider some things out of a Three-Man Rush Concept. The biggest problem with playing Zone Coverage is when we get into the Up Back situations where the linebacker is responsible for the curl. They are going to run a receiver in front of the linebacker and one behind him. If you do not want to play man-to-man you can do some things to help your defense.

Play Zone: Cover One Receiver Man-to-Man: This helps on read screens, floods, and option routes.

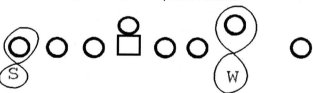

DOUBLE LEVEL DROPS

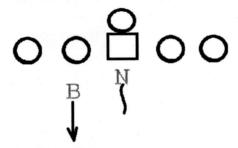

SHORT FLAT AND DEEP FLAT

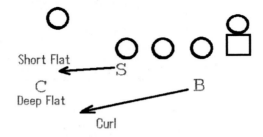

SHORT CURL AND DEEP CURL

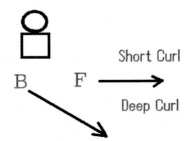

Let me get into some of our Special Pass-Rush Fronts. Generally we get into the even front and let them take off. It is a Speed Rush. It is a balanced four-man rush. Place the rushers in leverage positions. With wide rush lanes, we can twist on either side.

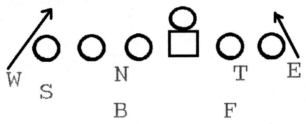

We have used the defense the Chicago Bears made famous where we cover the guards and put a man on the center. We still have the ability to rush the outside people. We have used this with different schemes. If we play against a center that is not a very good pass blocker, and we have a good nose man, we can apply pressure to the quarterback. You can isolate that center with a good nose man.

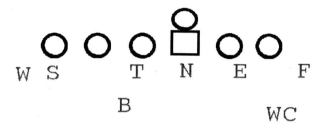

We have overloaded to one side like they do when they play touch football. It is a four-man rush with three rushers to one side.

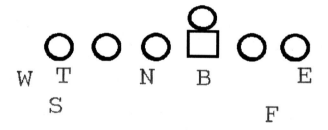

Through the years we have used the Bubble. We have dropped one man and used him on the run as well as on the pass. You can rush him or have him play an area or man.

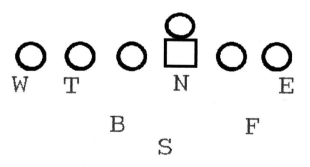

We have used the inside linebacker games. There are all kinds of arrangements on this. These are all drop-back pass coverages. When we do this, we give up a zone or play man-to-man.

If we want to bring perimeter pressure, we can do it with one linebacker. We give up a zone or play man-to-man. The secondary must be aware of what you are giving up. We have the ability to rush two people outside the offensive tackle on both sides. If we want to go to an overload we can occupy the center and send three people to one side. There are a variety of things you can do. It depends on what your problems are. You have to give up a zone.

I do not care what you do on defense, but it is very important to disguise it. We want to mix it up to keep them off balance. There are certain things you have to disguise to help your defense. You do not want the quarterback to be able to check out of a play and just raise up and throw the ball to the wide receivers every time you make an adjustment in your defense. Disguise becomes very important on any type of blitzing you do. You do not want them to predetermine when you are going to blitz by alignment.

We are seeing a lot of One-Back Offense. The things we are seeing as far as the running game are the Trap, Belly, and Toss to the tight-end side. We see some teams that give the fullback and zone block. We see some teams that run counter and misdirection plays.

In the passing game we are seeing four quick wide receivers. We are seeing a lot of bootlegs. Our basic adjustments would be to slide the linebackers to get into position to handle those receivers. We want to align so we can cover those receivers and still be able to cover the run. We want to be able to jam all four of those threats in the passing zone. We also want to be able to apply perimeter pressure because of all of the bootlegs we are seeing. Against Twins we are seeing teams that cross receivers. Some teams flood the area toward the Twins. We want to be able to apply some type of pressure to the Twins side of the formation. Against the Trip Sets we normally see the Drop-Back Passing Game. With the Slot on Trips, we are seeing reverses and things of that nature.

Chapter 13

DEFENSIVE SECONDARY TECHNIQUES

Rick Smith
University of Kentucky
1991

I have worked with a lot of great defensive coaches in my career. I have seen it all. I have been in every system in football. I have coached combination man-to-man, three-deep zone, and two-deep zone. I have had to coach all of this at the same time, which I am doing now at Kentucky. This is very hard. To have multiple fronts it is necessary to have a system to be multiple in the secondary as well. I have learned something from each defensive coordinator that I have worked for. One thing I learned from Rick Lantz 10 years ago was that every coverage has a theory. Before, the defensive lines did not understand that coverage, and at times the linebackers would not understand the coverage, either. When Coach Lantz would add a coverage he would always have the entire team together when he added a coverage. He would get up and explain the theory of that coverage. He would explain the entire defense to the entire team. He would give the whole team the complete picture of what the theory of the defense was. It gave everyone an overall understanding of the defense. Anytime we added a front to the defense he wanted the backs to see what the front was doing. We want our defense to have a total understanding of what we are doing. I have never forgotten that.

From Don Lindsey I learned that each coverage has a strength. Don't let the defense be defeated at the strongest point. If we are in a three-deep zone they better not hit a post or fade route on us. If we are playing a two-deep zone with 5 under, then they better not complete anything underneath on us. If they get deep on us someone did not do his job underneath. We try to make our players aware of the strength of each defense and we let them know we have called it for a reason. We also knew if every coverage had a strength, it also had a weakness. We want our kids to understand the weakness of each defense. When we put in a coverage we want them to understand the theory of the coverage and we want them to know the strength and weakness of the coverage.

About five years ago I went to a clinic in San Antonio, Texas, and Dave McWilliams was talking. Dave had just taken the job at Texas Tech, and is now the head coach at Texas. Dave is a super guy. He had on his blue jeans and had his chew of tobacco and his cigar. He was just a coach's coach. He was always sitting around talking with the high school coaches. I am happy now that they are having a lot of success at Texas. Dave talked at that clinic and I got one thing out of it that has stayed with me. He said, "Every coverage has to be adjusted." Football has changed so much in the last 10 years. Six years ago everyone in the Southwest Conference was running the option. Everyone had two backs in the backfield. Then when I got to Baylor they had gone to the one-back and no-back offense.

When we put in a coverage, I want my players to understand the theory of the coverage. When they understand the theory of the coverage, then I want them to understand that we cannot let the strength of that coverage be defeated. If the strength of the coverage is defeated then I have to get someone else in the game. If they get the bomb against us when we are in a 3 deep then someone is going to come out of the game. That is a cardinal sin to me in 3 deep. We gave up 3 fade routes in our 3-deep coverage because the corner did not do what he was supposed to do. When the corner does not do what he is supposed to do, then it means I did not do my job. That means that Larry New did not do his job. If we do not start doing our jobs then Bill Curry is going to get someone else to coach the defense. Larry New may end up getting someone to come in to do my job. "The crap rolls downhill." I tell the players that. "If you do not do the job then your butt is coming out. My family is important to me. My livelihood is coaching and we must play good for me to keep my job." They can understand this. So they learn that the strength of the coverage cannot be defeated.

Here is the weakness. If they figure out the weakness and defeat the coverage then we have to adjust the coverage. Once the players understand these theories about our defense we get into the nuts and bolts of the defense. This is where we cover the individual techniques of defense.

The first thing I go over with my players to start every spring and every season: What will I demand of you as a defensive back? The first thing I tell them is *No Loafing*. If they loaf I am going to get them out of the game. Next I tell them to be a competitor. Probably the reason I was hired at Alabama was because I would not agree with Ray Perkins in my interview. He asked me what I thought my job was as secondary coach. This was my answer: " My job is to teach my players to make good decisions most of the time. The way I teach them to make those good decisions most of the time is by the way I practice." Ray Perkins said, "I do not agree with you. You have to teach them to make the right decisions all of the time." I said, "If I tell them that, they will be afraid to make a mistake and they will play scared. I do not want anyone back there playing scared for me." We argued on this point for about 10 minutes. But this is the point I want to make: You have to be a competitor. You cannot be afraid to make a mistake. If you make a mistake, line up and play the next play. It is my job to make the players do their jobs right every time.

I tell them these points in that first meeting. I will accept nothing less than your best. I am a nice guy, but when I go on the field, I am all business. I will get mad and I will jump their butt. That is the way I coach, and I can't coach any different. I do not want any excuses. You either do it right or you do wrong. Don't give me any excuses. This next point is very important. I will not try to please my players. It is their job to please me. Some players think you are supposed to cater to them and be nice to them. I do love them to death. I treat them just like they were my own kids. I have three children of my own and when they do something wrong I chew their butts out. If they do something good I will hug them and love them to death. Get better each day. You never stay the same. Don't take chances. Make good decisions. That is my job, to teach them to make good decisions.

These are things that I expect on every play. Alignment; no mistakes on alignment. If you do not line up right, you can't do your assignment. Get into position to play. If you have to contain, contain. Contain means to keep the football inside and in front of you. If you are an alley layer, stay inside-out on the football. Tackle; any time the ball is thrown, plant, drive, and run to the ball, and take the proper pursuit angles. This may sound elementary, and I was taught this in high school 25 years ago, but it is still very important.

The last two points are very important:

1. What can I expect from you as a player? What can I expect from my players? Can I expect them to loaf? What can I expect from you on every play? Can I expect them to line up right?

2. Can I trust you as a player? How do you earn my trust? What does this mean? That means if we are playing cover 3 and you are playing the corner, are you going to stay deeper than the deepest man. Are you going to do what you are supposed to do on defense?

Next is a part of my philosophy on secondary play. These are some general things that I teach on defense. The first thing we do at UK is to swarm the football. What does this mean? It means they must give us 100 percent from the time the ball is snapped until the whistle blows. After every game our players are given a swarm grade. They get a plus or minus for effort on every play. When the game is over we come up with their overall percentage grade as a unit. They have to grade out 91 percent or better on swarm to be a winner for that game. We also do that with the linebackers and the front. We have a team swarm grade. One thing about our team is this. We may not have won a lot of games, but we damn sure ran to the football well and we got better each week.

There are two things that will get you in more trouble in the game of football than anything else. Those two things are your eyes and your feet. We spend hours on technique on this. I am on their butt all of the time about their feet and eyes. I am concerned about their feet in their stance, and where they are looking. If you don't have your feet right, you are dead. If you do not have your eyes right, you are not going to do what you are supposed to do. I ask my kids to see an awful lot when the ball is snapped. Eyes and feet are very important.

The two main functions of the secondary are these. First, no long passes. I believe we can limit all passes to less than 20 yards if we do what we are supposed to do. Every time we did give up a pass play over 20 yards someone screwed up. When you give up long runs of over 15 yards you are losing containment, someone is not keeping the ball inside the perimeter, or the alley man gets outside the ball, and you miss tackles. These are all errors on your part. We do not want to give up a run over 15 yards on defense.

There are two concepts of coverage on defense. I do not try to make it difficult. You are either playing a zone or man technique. You can play man, blitz man, combination man, you can play all zone, or you can play combination zone. Every coverage has a theory. I covered this with you; know it. Every coverage has a strength, a weakness, and an adjustment. Never let the strength of the coverage be defeated. Make them defeat the weakness of the defense.

There are four base coverage concepts. We teach our players two deep and three deep. Now, three deep does not mean that you have to rush four people. You can rush four, or drop four underneath, and have three deep. You can rush three and play five under zone, with a three deep. At Baylor against Houston we rushed two and dropped six, and played three deep. There are a lot of different ways that you can play three deep. It is the same on two deep. We can rush two, three, or four. You can play all kinds of combinations.

We also have man-to-man, combination man, and zone. The main two fundamentals of the secondary are tackling and catching of the football. They seem very elementary. I have a lot of techniques that I teach, but there are two fundamentals involved: tackling and catching the football.

At Baylor the year before, we had 23 interceptions. At UK last year we only had four interceptions. I started questioning my ability to coach the secondary. We went back and looked at the films and counted the number of passes that we dropped in the secondary. We counted 29 dropped footballs that could have been interceptions. If we could have only intercepted 50 percent of those 29 passes we would have been in the top 10 in the NCAA. The number 1 team in NCAA Division I only had 24 interceptions this year. If we could have intercepted half of those 29, we would have been up close to the leader.

The main four techniques we teach in the secondary are these. We have to teach them to play a one third deep, one half deep, how to play the flat, and we have to teach them how to play man-to-man. I start coaching technique before I tell them about a coverage. That is because we are so multiple. I will teach them all how to play each of the techniques. We can play the flat several ways. But, once they learn those four techniques, then when I tell them we are going to play a cover 3, and cover 8, you men play one third deep. Now they know the technique. If you are playing one half deep, it is cover 5.

I tell our players there are three types of routes in football. We play a lot of man-to-man at UK and when we play man we are reading the receiver. You are reading the receiver. If we are playing zone, we are looking at the quarterback. I want them to understand that football is not difficult. There are three types of routes they are going to run. I can't tell them if the receivers are going to run the pattern inside or outside, but they will run one of three types of routes. They will run a quick route, intermediate route, or a deep route. They can run one bastard route, which is the comeback route. If I am playing man, the first thing I have to defend is the three-step drop, which is the 5-yard out, or hitch, or slant route. For the man to run that route he has to show me something at 3 yards. As I am backing out on the play, the receiver's body language will tell me what he is going to do. If he drops his hips, his shoulders come up, and he takes those short, choppy steps, then he is fixing to break in or out. We try to read the stem of that release to see if there is a hint on his route, in or out. If he runs past the 3-yard depth, and gives no indication that he is running a quick route, then I must start thinking of the intermediate route. He is not going to break it off at 10 to 12 yards now. This means his body language must show me something at 8 yards. If the man is going to break it off at 10 yards, his body will give us a clue. He can't turn on a dime. He has to show us something at 8 yards if he is going to make a move. If he doesn't make his cut at 10 to 12 yards deep we back out of there. Now it is a deep route and he is going to run a fade, corner, or the post. If I am playing zone coverage in a three deep and I am playing the corner outside, I am thinking the same thing, but I am reading the quarterback. Does the quarterback set up at three steps? If he sets up at three steps, I know the man is running a quick route. If the quarterback goes back five steps it could be an intermediate route. It could be a deep route. If it is a quick route it must be thrown in 1.3 seconds. We teach them this and they understand the quarterback is trying to throw on rhythm. They throw in 1.7 seconds on a 10- to 12-yard route, and 2.5 seconds if it is a deep route. We also tell our defensive linemen this.

Adjustments have become one of the most important things I do as a secondary coach. People give you so many sets today. The thing that we have come around to is this. We tell them the first thing they must determine when they break the huddle is how many backs are in the backfield. If they have two backs in the backfield they could only possibly be in four formations. They could be in a pro set, with a tight end and flanker on the same side. It does not matter if the end is outside and the flanker inside, or the flanker outside and the end inside. To us that was a pro set. The slot was just the opposite. The tight end was by himself on one side. The reason this is important is because we may make a double call. But, if it is a standard pro set we are going to be in the first digit. If it is a slot set or a flip set we are going to be in the second digit called. There are four two-back formations that we care about. Out of those four, we are going to play first digit on three of them because it is the same as a standard set. There is only one set where we would play the second digit. This is where we start.

Against the one-back set we say there are three formations. First, is the balanced set with two receivers to each side. That is the same as a standards set, so we are in a first digit set. If they have three receivers on one side, and the backside receiver is split, then we treat that as a pro set and play first digit. The only time we would play the second digit against the one back set is if the tight end is by himself, and three men on the opposite side. The way we teach this is simple. We say that in every formation there are three receivers and two backs, regardless of who they have in the game. On one back we have doubles, rips, and trey. We treat the shotgun set the same as a pro set.

Now I will talk about technique. If you can play bump-and-run, and if you are as good as the receivers talent-wise, I would play bump-and-run on every down. This will encourage the offense to run the fade route. It takes longer to throw the other patterns. If we can line up in bump-and-run we have cut down on the things we have to defend as a defensive back. You have to spend time on keeping the man from releasing inside. That is the dangerous part of playing bump-and-run. We worked on the bump-and-run every day for 10 minutes a day at Baylor and at UK. I like the defense, but we just did not have the personnel to play it much at UK. I love the bump-and-run but you have to have someone to hit the quarterback. You should hit the quarterback if you play bump-and-run because you are going to send six rushers. If you are in a read blitz you could have seven on the rush. The more times you can hit the quarterback the more times that quarterback will be thinking about the rush and he will not set the back foot on his throw. If you do not have good athletes I would not play bump-and-run.

The first place I start is with a diagram on half coverage. We look at the diagram and see we have the half for the deep man real big. That is a real big area. It is from the middle of the field to the boundary. We have six zones underneath that we try to cover. We have three zones on each side of the ball. Out the outside we have the flat, next is the curl, and next is the hook closest to the ball inside. Here is where most teams try to attack this defense. They key to attack the corner fade route area to each side. Next, they attack with crossing routes with three vertical in the hold area. And they try to hit the fade in the other outside area. This is where we start teaching this defense. The theory of the coverage is that we are going to rush four, drop four players in the underneath zones, and play two deep players in the halves of the field.

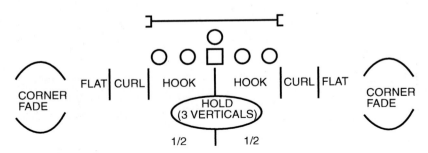

I tell them that I do not want any corner or fade routes completed against us. If they throw the ball to the flats against this coverage then they have a 6-yard gain. If they are 6-yarding us to death, then we will change the coverage. We will play a true hard corner and knock the man's head off and go down the road. That is a big area in the two-deep secondary. We tell them we have five men underneath. That is the strength of this coverage. Some people say that we should not tell the players that we have a weakness on this defense. I will tell them the weakness of the coverage is our two deep. I tell them the weakness for this reason. I want the other players to understand that those two-deep men cannot play halves back there without having pressure put on the quarterback. If we do not tell them this the corners and linebackers will not try to reroute the receivers. That is the reason we tell them our weakness on the coverage. That is Cover 1 in our terminology.

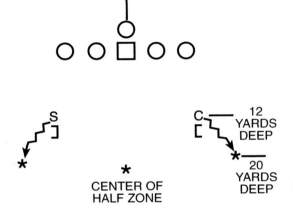

If I am playing halves I am going to start with their alignment. If the ball is in the middle of the field we show them how much area they have to cover. The zone for the safety is 27 yards wide. If you stand him in the middle of his zone he has 13 yards on each side of him. He has 13 yards to cover inside to the middle and 13 yards to cover to the sideline. His landmark is 4 yards outside the hash mark when he starts. He is 20 yards deep if the ball is off the line of scrimmage. He is lined up at 12 yards deep at the snap of the ball.

We line up on the hash mark if the ball is in the middle of the field. We line up 12 yards deep. I teach them to be comfortable. I want their hips and shoulders square to the line of scrimmage. I have had some players that wanted their feet parallel. That is fine with me. Others have wanted to drop their outside foot because that was the way their land mark was. They have a vision spot. The two deep backs have the same vision, but from opposite sides. We try to look into the backfield at a vision spot and I want them to see the entire picture. I do not just want them to see the quarterback. I do not just want them to just look at the tight end. I want them to see the entire picture. They can do that if you coach them. When the ball comes off the line of scrimmage that tells the defensive man to get back deep to his landmark as fast as he can. He must get his depth because he can't be beaten deep.

As he reads the ball off the line of scrimmage, which is the three lane to us, he must determine what the tight end and tackle showed him. The tight end can only do four things. If the quarterback is off the line, chances are he will not block. If the tight end does not block he is out of the pattern read for the deep back as the ball is off the line. Now he is only concerned with number 1 and number 2 to his side. The corner is only concerned with number 1 or number 2 to his side. If the tight end runs a drag, he can forget him. If he runs a flat, forget him. If he is vertical, don't forget him. When he is vertical he can press you deep and there is a chance they can get three deep receivers on us. I want to see all of this on the snap if I am playing the deep corner. I am working for my landmark.

If the tight end is flat in or flat out, then I will take a peek at the Z receiver, which is #1. I want to know if he released out or in. If the tight end made a flat in or flat out release, and I get an inside release, which I call a squeeze, by the Z back, then I cannot continue to gain width. He has to get depth and keep inside leverage on number 1 inside. If number 2 goes inside or outside and the tight end runs a fade route, the corner runs right through his landmark on his backpedal and eventually he will turn his hips and take the fade away.

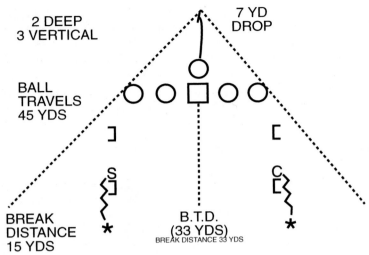

If he gets vertical from the receiver the corner can no longer get width. The landmark is the point that he starts to take away the fade, which is the toughest route he has to take away. He only runs to the fade if the tight end is not vertical, and the Z receiver runs the fade. If the tight end is inside or outside the only man he has to cover is the Z receiver. Now, he must determine if the Z receiver went inside or outside. He must know that. He has to position himself so he can cover one half of the field. He can't stand in the middle of the zone and cover those 13 yards. He has to position himself in that zone depending on what number 1 and number 2 do. He has to see the tight end and quarterback on the snap of the ball. Some players can look at the tight end and quarterback and tell what the wide receiver is going to do without looking at him. I have coached some other athletes that had to look at that wide out to find out what he was doing after he read the quarterback and tight end. It depends on their peripheral vision.

The thing that scares us on this defense is if the offense runs three vertical routes on us. They may run a fade on the two corners and send the tight end deep down the middle. This is what I try to sell them on this. For the quarterback to throw the ball to the fade on the boundary, the ball has to travel 45 yards. The longer the ball travels distance-wise, the more time we have to get there. If they throw the ball to the tight end it travels 33 yards. We tell our players they can cover one third the distance the ball travels. If the ball travels 30 yards the defensive back should be able to travel 10 yards. This will vary depending on the velocity of the quarterback's arm. I am talking about an average quarterback on this. If we see the ball come out of the quarterback's hand, and if we have great technique on our stop foot drive foot, we have a good chance to cover the 10 yards if the ball travels 30 yards. I use the chart to make them aware of how far they can travel, or move, to cover a given route. If they have a fade route to the sideline they can travel 15 yards on a pass that travels 45 yards. They have to be in a position in the middle of their zone so they are no further than 11 yards from the ball that is passed down the middle of the field. That is how we start on this defense. We want to know how the offense is going to take the weakness of this defense away.

If the ball is on the hash mark, the corner into the boundary, depending on the split of the wide receiver, he can line up on the hash mark or 2 yards outside the hash mark. If the receiver is outside the numbers, halfway between the bottom of the numbers and the sideline, we say that is normal. He can be 2 yards outside the hash mark. If he comes inside the numbers, then we will move back to the hash mark. A normal split to the wide side of the field is 1 yard outside, up to 2 yards inside the hash mark. If he is somewhere near the hash mark we are going to put our safety 12 yards deep, and 4 yards inside the hash mark. He has the same landmark. If the wide out is 2 yards wider, our safety is going to widen 2 yards which will put him 4 yards outside the hash mark. From the hash mark to the sideline is about 17 yards. If he is 4 yards outside the hash he has to break 12 yards to the boundary. They may not continue on that path. That is just a departed angle they start on when the ball is snapped if the quarterback is off the line of scrimmage. Again, this is if they read pass. Once they start their departure, where they end up depends on what the tight end and Z receiver do. They are concerned with number 1 and number 2. Now, for the quarterback to throw the fade route to the far sideline it must travel a long, long way.

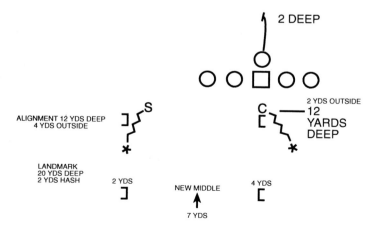

The Five Under Corners must see the same things as the safeties. We line them up 7 yards deep. At 7 yards deep we can disguise better, you can roll better, and you can play engage funnel better. We want the two corners to look inside, and they have the same vision spots that the safeties have. We teach them to read the triangle. They are looking at quarterback, near back, and tight end. We want them to make sure they know what is going on with the triangle, and if they do have to take a peek outside to see number 1 they can. If they can see that with their peripheral vision, then they can do that.

We line up 7 yards deep, and 1 yard outside. If we play a lot of man-to-man we are going to stay square to the line of scrimmage with the inside foot slightly back. If I am just laying zone a lot I want them turned inside. We want him to know what number 2 is doing, and what the quarterback is doing. He has to read; is the ball off the line, is it away from me, or is the ball to me, on the line of scrimmage, or off the line of scrimmage? On the snap of the ball, if the ball is in the three lane, and the tight end is inside, then I expect a great reroute by him. On the snap of the ball, he will read the backfield and punch, square up and start working back real slow as he reads the tight end on a drag pattern. He may be 9 yards deep now. Then he gets his head over on the outside receiver and he is going to mirror him. If he is outside he must shuffle outside. If he is inside, then has to shuffle inside.

When we tell them we want them to shuffle this is what we want. Shuffle means that they are moving parallel to the line of scrimmage. If we say shuffle zone, it means the man is shuffling with his butt to the boundary. We do not want the knees to cross in the shuffle. If we have to cross over to get a reroute we will. If the receiver is so wide that I can't get a jam on him without crossing over, I will turn and run and try to head him off at the pass. I may only be able to get one hand on him. I know I have to run 12 yards deep to stop the fade. If the ball is thrown on the fade he must come out of it and try to bat the ball down from the inside.

On the squeeze release we are going to look inside and see what we are supposed to see. We know what the tight end is doing. We know it is a pass. We snap our vision and look for number 1. That is the man we line up on. We want to shuffle inside and look for number 1. Most players want to cross their feet, and cross over and run. I tell them they cannot cross over until they have shuffled two or three times. As I shuffle I want to know what the departure angle of the receiver was. If he releases inside the 3-yard box, then I can get a hit on him as he comes off. If he releases outside the 3-yard box, I can't get a hit on him. If he releases outside flat, then he has already rerouted. He is not a threat for the safety if he reroutes to the flat. If he does that I can turn my butt to the boundary and shuffle zone. I face the quarterback with my back to the sideline. If I feel the ball is thrown, I turn and run to the fade area. We do not want the fade route to be completed. We are not going to give them anything. I will make them throw the ball short, and never give them the fade route. We tell the corner not to break down when he comes up to make the tackle. We tell him to come up and make paint splatter, but not to break down. We want him to go through the man. We want the receiver mashed. They may complete some of those flat routes on us, but they must complete five of those flat routes for one fade route. We do not just give them the flat route, but they may get a few of those on us. If we can take the flat route away from them we can call the cloud look and roll to three deep. We will tell the corner that we are going to roll the safety and he can go take the flat.

There are some change-ups that we use. We can run a switch call. Cloud means the corner has force. Switch means the safety has force. It depends on the strengths of the four athletes playing the corners and safeties as to what you can do.

If you are going to play a lot of cover 1 we help our players out as much as possible and play some three deep roll. If we are going to roll it weak, we try to beat the man inside and make a big play on the option. If we are rolling cover 3, and we are rolling and we see option we are not going to engage the blocker. Cover 9 is the same thing only it is called roll strong. We can roll either way.

QUESTION: How do we take on the lead blocker if the Z receiver were to crack block?

I tell him to get up the field. I want him to come up under control. I do not want him to come up and just smash it. I want him to come up the field and look at the man's head and earhole of his helmet. I want him to look at the blocker. I want him to get his outside foot back. Don't let the blocker reach his outside leg. He must get his hands down. I want one hand down on the blocker's helmet and one hand on the shoulder. One wants to take him on the inside leg up and try to push him to the ground and then shuffle with him. I try to keep the football inside. If the crack block comes toward me I am going to get up the field and take on the blocker. We work on the cut block every day. It is eyes, hands, and feet. You have to get your feet right and look at what you are supposed to look at.

One thing Coach Lantz taught me at Georgia Tech was to film from the ground to see if we have the inside leverage on the receivers. We cannot see that from up high. So one day we would film from the ground and then we would film from up high. If we are lined up inside we must work to keep that leverage if the man comes inside on us. In man-to-man you have to take one or the other positions away from the receiver. If you are inside and they throw the out pattern, you have to make the play. You have to take the inside or outside away in man.

We do a lot of drills. I have a set of drills that I do on Monday and a set that I do on Tuesday. Every day after practice, when they are tired, we have four drills that we use. In the second half they are tired and we want them to do the drills to help them in the game. We do the stop-foot drive-foot drill, and we do the M drill that they hate. If I can get them to do it right after practice I can get them to do it right in a ballgame.

Chapter 14

SECONDARY TECHNIQUES AND DRILLS

Jon Tenuta
Ohio State University
1998

There are phases that people look at in coaching the secondary. The first thing is philosophy. The second one is your plan of attack based on who you are going to play. The third one is what coverage you are going to play based on formation. You must have a plan of action that deals with your forcing unit.

The first thing that I'm going to start with is what we call "Defensive Back Checkpoints." It is a list of things we talk about even before we go to practice. The first thing we talk about is Vision. Vision is the indispensable tool of the secondary player. This starts before the snap and carries through the play. I stay after my players about having tunnel vision. They have to see the receivers, the whole formation, and what is going on before the snap. We try to instill in our players to keep their eyes and feet alive at all times.

The second thing we talk about is the Stance. A proper stance will help you to be physically and mentally alert. Obviously every individual is different. We would like to have 12 cloned safeties and corners. It doesn't happen. Last year I had Sean Springs. He was 6-0 and 192 pounds and ran a 4.3 40. This year I had Antawn Winfield, who was 5-8 and weighed about 170 pounds. Those two guys' stances are not going to be the same. The way they backpedal is not going to be the same. One of them had a long stride and the other had a short one. When you look at the stance, we want it as compact as possible. We want the shoulders over the toes. The knees should be bent and they should glide in the backpedal.

The next thing is Footwork. The secondary players must be able to break and make cuts going backward and forward. Secondary coaches should spend as much time as possible working on transition. That is working on coming out of the backpedal to break on a ball or reacting to the run. This has to be worked on all year. They have to work during the season as well as in the off-season on the transition phase of their game. That is one thing our guys do a great job of. They work on their backpedal and transition, so they can get quicker at getting to the junction point.

The fourth thing we talk about is Quick Reflexes. This is the ability to move your body or parts of it more quickly than the next man in a restricted area. That comes to bear in the one-on-one coverage.

The next thing we look at is Tackling. We must be sure tacklers. You don't have to blow the guy up, you just have to get him on the ground. We spend more time tackling than most teams do. But we are firm believers that you've got to live to play another down. We talk about these things in our tackling drills. Look at the man at the moment of contact, explode, and accelerate your feet. This goes back to vision. In spring practice we make our defensive backs say "Eyes, Eyes, Eyes!", before they make a tackle. The defensive backs have to excel in open-field tackling. They should gather themselves slightly before making the tackle. We don't want them out of control so they can't make the play. Never dive unless you are going over a man or obstacle or a last-chance effort. It has happened to everyone. It happened to us last year and it cost us. They just threw their bodies as a last-ditch effort. If they had taken a few more steps they could have made the play.

Always keep proper pursuit angles and position. The one thing we spend a lot of time on is angle and position in pursuit. We emphasize the proper angle so we can make that play when someone else gets blocked.

The sixth thing is Defeating Blocks. We must be able to meet and defeat blocks. We have to play high, low, and lead blocks, and stay on our feet. We are no different than defensive linemen and linebackers. We have to get ourselves into a position to defeat the block and make the tackle.

Playing the Ball is the next thing we cover. Always be rough and aggressive when you make a play on the ball. We are going to be intimidating secondary players. When the ball is in the air we are going to become the player who wants the ball the most. We play the ball at its highest point. Go up with two hands and break up a pass. If the defensive back can get two hands on the ball, we want the interception. If you can't use two hands, use one hand and knock the ball down toward the ground. Converge on the ball once it is in the air. The defensive backs have equal rights to the ball. They need to play rough and hard. People are going to catch the ball on you. But we stress no yardage after the catch.

When we talk about Zone Coverage, it is the area where a player has to cover. The first thing we talk about in the pre-snap read is how many threats do you have by formation that can threaten your zone. We play zone about 35 percent of the time. With two men in your zone, always defend the deepest first. Never give up the home-run ball. Keep your eyes and feet alive. When I am in the zone I want to see the quarterback getting ready to throw the ball and also see where the receiver is. I want to see the receivers break and see the ball thrown. We want to have a clear picture of the quarterback's front shoulder. We are not going to break until the ball is released. But our guys know when the eyes and the front shoulder open to the target, that is our key to get ready to break on the ball. There are no excuses for a "Bomb."

The ninth thing is Man Coverage. Man is where a defender is man-for-man with his opponent all over the field. We play a lot of man coverage at Ohio State. We spend a lot of time in pure man coverage against our own receivers. It has paid off greatly for us. It paid off for Sean Springs because he had the opportunity to go against Joey Galloway and Terry Glenn. The more repetitions you have in man coverage, the better back you are going to be. In man coverage proper footwork and position are the most important things. The defensive back must stay balanced and work for position on the receiver. He has to get the position first and then look and lean for the ball. One thing we work on at Ohio State is staying in our backpedal as long as we can. If a back is not hip to hip and looking in the receiver's earhole on the headgear, then he is not in position to look for the ball. If he isn't in that position the only thing he has left is to tackle the receiver after he catches the ball.

The last thing that we talk about is Refine your Technique. That to us means to upgrade your play every day. A lot of guys do some things well. We want to work on our weaknesses and not our strengths. Your kids have a starting point for what you as the coach are looking for.

Once we go out to practice the first thing we do in the secondary is backpedal across the field. I line up on the boundary line and the safeties and corners line up on the numbers. They backpedal down the yard lines across the first hash mark and the second hash mark. Once they get to the far numbers, they can relax. We do that to go through our checkpoints. We check the stance, balance, and habit. Habit means I want them to backpedal the same way in the first quarter as they do in the fourth quarter. For us to be successful at Ohio State, we have to get into a habit that can't be broken. The reason I use the lines is to keep them straight as they backpedal. Once they get across the field, my graduate assistant sends them back to me. If you video the backpedal, you can find the things you need to work on.

We have all types of drills that we work on going across the field. The next one is the 45-degree break for posts and corner routes. What I like to work on is keeping them as a unit. I backpedal them, let them read my front shoulder, and then drive them at a 45-degree angle getting depth. I can work a number of people on this drill instead of one at a time. Again, backpedal them down the line and break them at 45 degrees, which gives them an aiming point.

The next thing we work on is the Dig and the Out. It is the same drill as the 45-degree break except we break on a 90-degree break. They backpedal down the line and break on the shoulder at a 90-degree break. These are the routes they are going to have to defend when they make this kind of break. We tell the safeties they are working on the Dig route and the corner is working on the Out route. That is what they see.

The next move is what we call Downhill. When we work on this move it is just as much a zone move as it is man technique. We backpedal our backs down the line. We make them change direction and come forward without drop stepping or losing any ground to come forward. We want that smooth transition from backpedal to forward run. We can bring them back straight ahead or on a 45-degree angle.

The W Drill is something we do every day. That is a man-read drill. In this drill you backpedal, come forward on a 45-degree angle, and repeat the drill. Everything is done with a read. Because once we get out

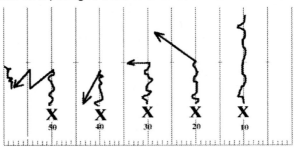

of the individual period we are going one-on-one against the receivers. This drill applies to our safeties in Cover 2 more than our corners.

The next thing we do is tackle. At Ohio State, before special team period begins, we have an agilities period for all players. During this period we do some loosen-up drills and get our players ready to go. From there we go to a tackling drill. Our defensive backs are going to tackle the wide receivers or the running backs. The linebackers are going to tackle running backs or tight ends. The defensive line tackles each other. The first tackling drill that the defensive backs do is a Goal-Line Tackling Drill. The tackler puts his heels on the boundary line. There are two cones placed 5 yards away from him to each side. The idea is for the running back to come downhill at that cone. The defensive back has to knock the crap out of him. When we go against each other it is a fit-up drill. When we go against the running backs or tight ends it is live and wide open. In the live drills we put the runner on the ground. The fit-up drills we don't. We spend as much time in the fit-up drills as we do with anything else.

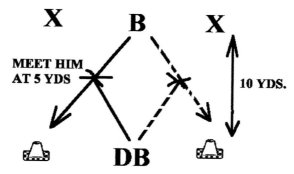

The drill we spend most of our time on is the Angle or Open-Field Tackling Drill. We do this every day. We work this drill between the hash marks. The ball carriers are on one side and the tacklers are on the other. The ball carrier is running downhill to the bottom of the

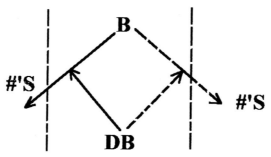

numbers. The defensive back has to be at the junction point 5 yards away and knock him back. We do not take the running back to the ground. There are no cutback seams for the back. He has to try to outrun the defensive back.

The next thing we do is create the same drill, except we tell the back he can go anywhere he wants. He has to start in one direction, but after that he can make as many moves as he wants. The bottom line in the drill is to get the running back on the ground.

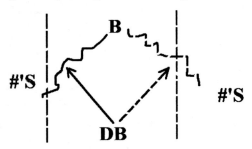

The third tackling drill we do is called Funnel Tackling Drill. The funnel tackle is based on our support scheme. We are going to show the safety in the diagram. He is 10 yards from the dummies which mark the alley. The ball carrier is 7 yards from the dummies. The dummies represent the C Gap. The safety had to come up and be in position to meet the running back in the funnel. Obviously he can't meet him in the hole, but he has to stay on his outside and make the tackle in the funnel. We are trying to make the tackle for a 2-to 3-yard gain.

We run the same drill for the corner. The only difference is he is coming from the outside of the funnel instead from the inside of the funnel. The corner wants to come up in the funnel and make the tackle. If he misses or loses the tackle he wants the ball carrier to have to go back inside. He has to close and make the play. He can't allow the back to have a two-way go. We spend a lot of time on this in our fit drills.

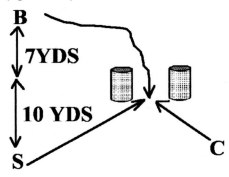

The next drill is a catching drill. The first catching drill is called Deep Ball Drill. Our players love this drill. We put the safeties on the hash marks and the receivers down on the numbers. The receivers run down the numbers and look back inside to me. The safeties are up at the hash marks. I throw the ball downfield and everyone goes after the ball. This is our zone concept. The ball may be thrown behind them, over them, or anywhere on the field. They have to react and go to the ball aggressively. You have to defend the deep ball, so we spend a lot of time doing it. We spend a lot of time getting our backs to turn a 180-degree turn and run straight lines down the field. If it is a zone coverage, the back tilts his hips to the quarterback. If it is man coverage he tilts his hips to the receivers.

During this time we work on our one-on-one coverage. We take a receiver and put the defensive back in a trail position on him. The receiver runs down the field with the back in the hip position. The back is running with the receiver looking in the ear hole of his head-gear. When the ball is thrown, the back gets his hands into the hands of the receiver and looks for the ball. The corners and safeties do this drill. We work this drill with the fade in the red zone also.

During these drills every day we will handle all breaks. We work on the out, dig, post, and post corner every day at some point in these catching drills.

The third drill we talk about is a Combat Drill. I line the safeties or corners up on the hash marks. They start off in a backpedal. I tap the ball and they turn inside and run. I throw the ball up for grabs and they go get the ball. You would be surprised who comes up with the ball. This drill is who wants the ball the most. I don't want them knocking the ball down. I want them to go up with both hands and catch the ball. If the ball goes on the ground they go again. Some-body has to come up with the ball.

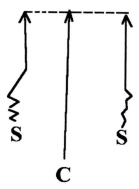

From there we go to defeating blocks. Our safeties play more blocks than the corners. The secret to playing blocks is not to get knocked off your feet. We set the drill up so the defensive back has to play off the block of a fullback or guard.

We have to learn to play the stalk block. The thing we have to learn is to lock up on the blocker. From there we learn to Rip with the same arm and same hip to get by the blocker and into position to make the tackle.

The third thing we work on in defeating blocks is the Spill Technique. If we have a 5-8, 170-pound corner who has to play a 300-pound pulling guard, we use the spill technique. All he does is take the knees of the blocker out. The defensive backs come on a 45-degree angle into the alley, take down the man pulling, and give the running back no cutback. We want everything spilled to the outside.

The last thing we talk about in playing blocks is the Last Man Drill. This is a drill where there is a ball carrier, blocker, and a defensive back. The defensive back has to make the tackle. If he is close to the boundary, he tries to force him into the boundary. He has to give ground as the blocker runs at him. We run this drill about three times in the spring and two times in the fall. The defensive back has to use his hands to play off the blocker and make the tackle. We work on this. We don't want to give ourselves up and give up a cheap touchdown. If the defensive back can buy some time the pursuit may come up to help him.

Our off coverage is probably no different that anyone else's. We are going to take away the inside by alignment. That is the easiest throw for the quarterback. When we play off the man we play it at 6 yards. I am fortunate to have guys who can play at 6 yards. Most people play at 7 to 8 yards. We are going to slow pedal through the three-step drop and maintain a livable and lateral cushion on the inside of the receiver. When we weave to maintain our inside position we try to keep our shoulders square and stay in a backpedal as long as we can. We takes pairs of backs and work on weaving back and forth and maintaining the inside position. The first thing we do in the spring is to test our backpedal. We put our defensive backs in the 6-yard cushion. The receiver takes off as fast as he can. The defensive back has to slow pedal through the three-step area before he gets into his speed backpedal. The defensive back is going to see how long he can stay in his backpedal before the receiver runs by him. Every defensive back knows where his break box is and where his transition takes over. Everyone is different. Sooner or later you are going to run by a guy like Sean Springs, but it may be 25 yards downfield. We read inside hip. If the hip disappears it is an inside throw. If he moves outside it is an outside throw. If the back is not sure, he maintains inside leverage.

We work a lot on our press technique. We use this technique when the back doesn't think he can get his hands on the receiver at the line of scrimmage. The receiver is off the ball and the defensive back may not be able to get his hands on the receiver. He may be too quick or have too many moves for the back to get contact on him. We play the press technique from an off position. We give ground and nail the receiver in the Break Box. As the receiver tries to get away from the back, he gets into the trail position on him. Now the back is hip-to-hip looking into his ear hole. His inside hand is going to be his steer hand. He drops it onto the hip of the receiver so he can feel his moves. This keeps him from losing contact and avoids separation with the receiver.

From there we go to bump-and-run or man technique. The defensive back knows he is going to get his hands on the receiver. The inside hand is going to be his steer hand. If the back steps at the receiver, he can easily become a trailer running for his life trying to catch up. He jams his hand into the pectoral area. By sticking the receiver, the back can open his hips, steer the receiver the way the back wants him to go, and flare his hip into the receiver. Now he has a chance to cover the receiver.

I want to talk about zone coverage. The first thing we have to be concerned with is threats. The first thing we have to recognize is the number of immediate threats to the defensive back's zone. In a regular formation if I am the strong safety, I see two threats. As the strong safety drops into coverage he is reading the patterns of his threats.

We don't just tell him that he has an area of responsibility, we make him aware of the patterns that are coming. We pattern read and put ourselves in positions to play routes. We work on one side at a time and work on the progressions of patterns on that side.

Chapter 15

TEACHING DEFENSIVE TEAM CONCEPTS

Dick Tomey
University of Arizona
1995

Fellows I'm going to go real fast. I want to take about the first half and just talk about some general things and the last half talking about our defense if we have time.

We believe you can build a team. We believe the most important thing in building a team is attitude. It is not Xs and Os. We work our buns off to build the right attitude. Being able to communicate as a coaching staff is important. Being able to communicate as a coaching staff to the players is also important. We try hard to build some relationships within our coaching staff. We start each summer with a retreat for our coaching staff. We go up in the mountains around Tucson for three days. We don't talk about football. We talk about philosophy, what we believe in, our own personal experiences, and our own lives. After dinner on that first night, each coach gives us his whole life story. He talks about his successes, failures, marriages, divorces, ups, downs, sickness, good health, or whatever he wants to talk about. He gives us all a look at him. The next night all of us ask each other questions based on what we heard the night before. These are probing kinds of questions. One of our coaches has had leukemia. We ask him how he handled that and how he battled back from that. This retreat is a start of communication for us as a coaching staff. We go out in the woods for walks and spend time with one another.

I have a very structured evaluation session with my assistant coaches. I sit down with each coach on my staff. I give them a form which is titled, "How do you see yourself?" They fill out the form. It is how

173

they see themselves in a variety of different areas. Some of the areas are on-field duties, off-field duties, their ability to relate to players, their players' performance, and things like that. I want to know their goals for next year. I want to know how they plan to achieve these goals. I also want them to critique me. How can I make their job easier? What can I do to be more effective as a head football coach? Some of us have a hard time sitting down with a peer, looking him in the eyes and telling him what you think. Go back in your mind and think how good you are at doing that. I think that is important to be able to do those things and handle them. As a staff we have to understand we have to communicate those tough issues within the staff with each other. These are some of the things we try to do to bring our staff together. To get close as a staff, you have to get under each other's skin. You can't have closeness if all you do is talk about football or stuff that doesn't matter. In order to get close to a player or coach you have to get inside of them. You have to talk about real issues, things that hurt, and things that are meaningful.

As far as the players go, to get to their gut-level issues, you must allow them into yours. If you are not willing to let them inside of you, you can forget about getting inside of them. You can't be a guy who is just there from 8 o'clock to 5 o'clock. You have to have them into your home, with your family, and be part of your life, if you want to be a part of their lives.

We try to have balance on our staff. We want a balance in experience. We have to have young guys and older coaches. We have to have creative coaches and conservative coaches. We have to have all kinds of different voices in the room if we want to have the right kinds of results.

The bottom line for building a team: If you want the results on the field as far as performance, you've got to have a family. You have to have as much like a family situation as you can possibly get. Families fight, argue, and misunderstand one another. Football teams and coaching staffs do the same thing. If you are a family, you can fuss and fight. But when that is over, you can kiss and make up. To do that your players have to know you care.

We talk all the time as a coaching staff about how we are going to coach our team. We have a staff philosophy to deal with that. We actually care about these guys that play for us. We care for them not only when it is convenient for us. For 18 years I'm the only football coach in America who does not have an unlisted telephone number. I've never had one. Players need to get hold of you at 3 o'clock in the morning. They never seem to need you at 5 o'clock in the afternoon. They need you at 2 o'clock in the morning. Something has happened. It is probably not very pretty. But that is when they need you. Something is bothering them and they can't sleep. They need to talk and you need to be available for them. You have to have a family and we are committed to that.

I believe great coaches like John Wooden or Bobby Knight are very different in the way they portray themselves. But they are very similar in the way they coach. They care, are consistent, and are highly competent. If you do what they say, you will have a chance to be successful. To me, I think that is what great coaches do. You don't change with the weather or a win or a loss. You don't believe in somebody one day and not believe in him the next. Those are what we call the "Three Cs" of coaching. Caring, consistency, and competence are the "Three Cs." This is the way we're going to coach. As a coaching staff you have to decide how you're going to coach, the way you are going to coach, and what you are going to coach. After that you just do it. You have to deliver that to the young guys you are working with. You want them to believe in you. Belief is the most powerful thing in the world. They have to believe in themselves, you, the coaching staff, in what you are doing, that they are going to win, fight, and bust their butts. They believe. They have to believe that in the game some Wildcat is going to make a big play and that Wildcat is going to be me. It is not going to be somebody else. They think that way because we teach it. That is part of the team thing. Belief comes from common sacrifice for a goal. We have to trust one another and communicate.

Sometimes you have to take some time and talk to everybody. At the University of Arizona and at Hawaii, I have felt compelled to have a marathon meeting. Sometimes it is important to talk to everybody and do it right now. It can't wait. We need to do it right now. We have to talk to every guy for as long as it takes. A couple of times we have done that, it has taken about 16-18 hours. It's like Coach Synder said: If you've got a problem, solve it right now. I have guys sign up four times. I will be there in the office for as long as it takes. I want to sit down and get eye-to-eye with them. I want to find out what's in their minds right now. I want them to see how I feel about the problem as well. Maybe they need to know you believe in them. Every single guy needs to know that. You don't necessarily believe in them as a football player. We have to be real about this thing. I believe in some of our guys as football players and some of them as people. Those people have not demonstrated yet that I should believe in them as a football player. They are working hard and going in the right direction, but they are not there yet. They have to earn the belief as a football player. But it will come.

A couple of years ago we had high expectations going into our season. We thought we were going to be a real good team. We played a couple of games. We won one and lost one. We went up to Oregon State, which at that time was a struggling football team but was getting better. We ended up tied that game. You know how it is when everybody expects you to be better than you are at that time. When we walked off the field and in the locker room, I've never seen such desperation in a football team. There was nothing in their faces. It was like someone had just stolen the most valuable thing they had. They had lost their pride. As a coach, you probably have seen that. As a coach you don't know what to do or say. I've got to get these guys feeling better about themselves, but at the same time make them understand they have just laid an egg. When we get home everybody will be shooting bullets at us from all different sides. I have to get the guys to leave the locker room with some feeling that they can be something.

I went outside and talked to my coaches. As I watched the guys coming out of the locker room, I didn't like the looks on their faces. I told my assistants to get them off the bus and send them back to the locker room. I got them back into the locker and told them a story about the same thing that happened at Hawaii. That team came back to go 8-3 and have a fantastic season. I told them that this Arizona team could do the same thing if we stayed together and believe in each other. I gave it my best shot and they looked a little better. But I still didn't like it. We got on the bus and started to the airport. I walked around the bus and guys looked like someone had just shot their mother. I told the pilot I wanted to get all the athletic boosters, directors, and people like that off the plane and get the team on so I could talk to them again. We got the boosters off the plane and then the team got on the plane.

I started again. "The looks on your faces were not the look of someone who was determined to do something. It was a look of a whipped dog. I wanted that look of not being able to wait until we played again." I didn't even know who we played next. Well it happened to be the University of Miami, in Miami. No one had beaten them there in 50 games. Their looks got better and we went home to Tucson.

When we had our staff meeting on Sunday, I told the coaches to go to work on Miami, I was going to meet with the team members. I wanted every one of them in my office; I wanted them to go with me on a walk and talk. I think guys relax when you go for a walk. I think guys will tell you what they really think when you go for a walk. Sitting in that office can be intimidating to them. The community couldn't wait to criticize the coach and players. I wanted the other message about believing to get to them. I wanted a personal commitment from each player to give more. All our guys made that commitment. We played Miami and they beat us 8-7. We kicked a 51-yard field goal as time expired that would win the game. It was a great kick but just wide and we got beat. They came off the field and now we have another problem. Everyone was excited because we only lost by a little bit. Now we have to talk about not taking any consolation about the fact we only lost by a little. But we could feel good about the effort, about the seeds sown here tonight for next week, and played well against a good team. The next week we played UCLA, which was ranked seventh in the nation. To make a long story short, we won seven of the last eight, finished second in the conference, and had a great year. To turn it around these guys had to have the right stuff in their hearts and minds.

During that same year we went out to practice one day and guys started to come late to practice. I was having a conniption fit. We had 16 guys late to practice. The truth of the matter was there was some kind of lab that afternoon. I told our team the number 16 is significant. When we play the University of Washington this week, we are going to play like there are 16 guys on the field. We played Washington, who was number 1 in the country, and won 16-3. The next day in the paper, their quarterback was quoted as saying "there seemed to be 14 of their guys on the field." We put that on the locker-room wall. Sometimes you can make a positive out of a negative.

We don't always get the job done. I thought this year we did a poor job of coaching. We lost the conference championship to Oregon 10-9. We didn't handle the expectations well at all. We didn't get their attention like we needed to. When I am talking I look for guys who nod their heads. I am looking for guys that are concentrating on what I am saying. Those are the guys that are tuned in. They are trying to understand. Guys that believe and want to believe.

We have three things we say as a coaching staff. These are absolute things I say to our coaches and there are no discussions about this. If you can't decide whether to hug a guy or kick him in the butt, hug him. If you can't decide whether your team is not tough enough and you're trying to decide to hit or not to hit, you hit the crap out of them. If your guys seem tired and you can't decide whether to rest or practice, we rest. We are going to hug them, hit them, and rest. If there are any questions, that is what we are going to do.

There are certain times as coaches, we have to say, "I don't care how you feel, we are going to do it this way." You have to have a combination of balance with those things. Building a team is the whole thing, not building an offense or defense. We do a lot of "One Fail All Fail." If we have a meeting and someone is late, everybody is up running the next morning. Same thing with the bed check. In our underwear we are all up running. We did that in training camp two years ago. One guy was late so everyone was in the mud, in their underwear doing 111 up-downs. That was one for every guy on the team. When you start playing your first game, if one guy screws up, we all suffer. We are no stronger than our weakest link. I am depending on you.

In building a team, sometimes you have to create a crisis to get a result. If you have a sore on your arm, it is not going to get well unless you rub it raw and let it bleed. Sometimes if you have a problem, you have to just let it go and create a mutiny. Get it in the open and get it solved.

We had an experience my first year at the University of Arizona. They had a good football team the year before and had great expectations for the coming year. I came in from the University of Hawaii and the WAC conference. I wore flip-flops and a Hawaiian shirt and they thought I was not tough enough and too relaxed. We started out all right but then we lost a game at Washington State. We didn't deserve to win the game. After the game I told the coaches to hang on because we were going to have a crisis right here. We may lose this whole year right now, but we are going to find out. I told the equipment man to turn the heat up in the locker room as high as it would go. We were going to stay in the locker room and cook these suckers. They were not going to play like that. I made them keep their pads on and I talked for 45 minutes. I started with "You guys think you are winners? Bull crap! There ain't a winner in the bunch. You wouldn't recognize one if he came through the door. You are thinking about last year and wishing you had last year's coach! Well you got us and you're damn lucky! We are going to practice tomorrow, which is Sunday, at 7 in the morning. We aren't going to get home until 1 a.m. and if anyone is late for practice they can pack it in." I told them I didn't care if they were All-American last year or not. You miss practice tomorrow and you're through at Arizona. Seven o'clock the next morning they were all there. Down deep they were there because they wanted to get better. They just needed somebody to get rid of that last-year stuff. It gave some guys the chance to do what they had been saying in private. We created the crisis.

We had gone through a long winning streak of about 12 games, and finally got beat by UCLA on national television. We didn't play well and our guys didn't handle it very well. We had a team meeting on Monday. It was awful. We had guys pointing fingers at each other and blaming everyone for the loss. I told the coaches we were not going to practice. We would just let it go. Every now and then I would go into the locker room just to see if there were any bodies to be taken away. Some of the leaders came out and wanted me to come in. All these emotions were coming out but what they were saying is they really cared about the team. They just didn't know how to express themselves. To make a long story short, we had the best team in the history of the school last year. The good thing is you can feel good about the fact you feel so bad.

Players are a mirror of their coach. Don't tell me that somebody got us beat because he didn't do something right. If they are coached in a disciplined manner, to respond to discipline, understand discipline, then they will play disciplined football. If they are coached to give great effort, they will give great effort. If they are coached fundamentally, they will play with great fundamentals. We all have to accept that. It is kind of scary. If you want to find out what kind of coach you are, turn on the film and look at it. Sometimes we like what we see and sometimes we don't. Some coaches give clinic speeches about things they don't do. If something happens on the film more than once, you are either coaching it or allowing it to happen. Both of these things are wrong. As a head coach, we give credit to the team and assistant coaches when we win. When we lose, the head coach takes the responsibility because people think it is your fault anyway.

Our teams at Hawaii and Arizona have been teams that played good defense. Four years ago we had a team where everybody got hurt. That was my favorite team because of the way they fought adversity. We beat USC in the second-to-last game of the season. We started four true freshmen on the offensive line, a freshman quarterback who was a tailback, and four linebackers, who at the start of the year were playing another position. In that year we departed from our regular defense and went to the defense of the week. We would end up one week having two linebackers or two down linemen. We tried to play what we had. From that season we went back to what we had believed previously. We need to line up in one defense and execute. The multiple defense was not our defense. We believe in lining guys up in the same place time after time and letting them get good at it. We believe in extreme simplicity. We wanted to take a look to see what would make our defense better.

What we came up with was a hybrid of some packages we have run over the years. We have been successful. We were the number 1 defense in college football last year in rushing defense, and have been close to the top the last three years. We were the number 2 team in scoring defense the last three years. We were number 3 in total defense the last three years. In our defense we only need two guys who are big strong guys. We have short guys. We have one guy in our huddle who is taller than 6-1. We would like to have a guy 6-5 and 280 pounds who can move, but we just can't get them. You don't have to be tall to play our defense, but you do have to be able to run. You have to play with great enthusiasm and love to play.

We demand certain attitudes on defense. We have to get the right kind of players on our defense. You must have the right personality. We have some crazy guys on defense that become infectious the way they play. They have that look in their eyes, where you are not quite sure what they are going to do. You have to have some of those guys, but you put them on defense. You have to make personnel decisions, which gives you a chance to have a good defense. If you are going to have a good defense, your signal calling on offense has to be good. You can't have three passes and out right before the half and help your defense. That is a sore subject with Dallas Cowboys fans. You have to have a scheme that allows flexibility. We play the same scheme all the time. It is great against Wishbone, No Backs, Three Backs, Cover Downs, and Cutback runs. Our scheme is a little crazy and unique. Not many people play it.

Can you fix it when it is broken? That is important in great defensive play. You have to know what happens to you and know how to fix it. If you have too much in your defensive scheme you can't do that. If you got too much you are just lucky if you play well. You have to fix it in the middle of the game.

Does your defense give your players an opportunity to turn it loose and have fun? In order to do that you have to be simple, so they know what to do. In the last three years, this last year was the worst defense we've played. We allowed 15 points a game and were second in the nation in rush defense. We did some good things. In the bowl game we allowed 75 yards. The longest drive against us was 18 yards. That team was averaging 500 yards a game. The bad news was we lost the damn game. We dropped a couple of passes and they returned a kickoff on us. The defense can play loose if they know what they are doing.

If you have a simple plan you can focus on teaching because they know where to line up. You can work on reaction to blocks and schemes because your players are going to align the same all year long. All people block us the same way. We can drill that to our kids over and over again. There are certain things against our defense that are not any good. We have a list of things that hurt our defense and we work on them.

We demand that our players do it right with great effort. Effort is the thing we are fanatical about. We don't want token or just good effort. We want great effort. We are fortunate to have enough guys on our team who did that when they walked into our place. We saw it on film when we recruited them. Some guys have no idea what great effort is. When you find it, make a training film out of it. One of those guys is 6-0 and 250 pounds. He has a great motor. His motor started running when he took the practice field and it ran all the time. When a defensive player changes direction we talk about explosion. We talk about noticeable change in mobility. It is not a smooth change. You can see it on the film.

Conditioning is important. We demand it, coach it, and grade it. If a guy plays 14 plays he is graded on his effort. If he has efforts against him, he works them off. A guy will run out in the middle of a group of guys and say, "My name is Dick Tomey and I've got two too many efforts! I'm going to do 10 up-downs for each one I've got!" "My name is Jim Hoffman, I've got 10 too many efforts for not pursuing the receiver after the ball was thrown! You're doing 10 up-downs because of me and that is the last time you'll do that!" When you grade effort you cut no one any slack. In the last game of the season we had only eight efforts to do. In the first game of the season we may have 40 to do.

Your players must be rested on game day to give great effort. That is something we all understand and realize. You can't go if you are not fresh.

When we were trying to put together a package and plan that we could understand, we had to make it simple. The first thing we wanted to do was stop the run. That is the most important thing in playing defense. When we were playing Coach Bill Walsh of Stanford, the first thing we had to do was stop the run. We want them to throw the ball every down. We wanted them to go to pure pass and then we sic the dogs on them. That makes them a predictable offense. You don't want to play a two-dimensional offense.

We have to be able to cover down formations. We have to have a defense that can adjust. When people start to go to Trips, No Backs, and offensive sets like that, we have to be able to adjust. We have a system that can do that as well as take the cutbacks away. When you cover down you can't create all kinds of gaps in your defense.

We want our presnap look to look the same for every defense we run. Whether it is man or zone or first down or third down, I want it all to look the same. The defense will look different if you are in Trips as opposed to Three Backs, but the defense is the same defense. We cover down the same way all the time.

You have to believe in man-to-man coverage. We play man-to-man coverage on every down. We play zone every down. But you have to believe in man coverage. You have to believe you can walk up, press people, and get right in their face. We minimize checkoffs.

Those are the things we felt we had to do to develop a package we could live with. In our front the linebackers are the adjusters. We liked the Chicago Bears' defense. But we didn't want to play it because we didn't feel it was sound against everything. We are going to play a 0 noseguard. We want to stop the cutbacks, so we put two people in sort of an eagle position. The tackle is in so wide a 3 technique that the guard can't cut him off. He is reading the hip of his guard so if he blocks down he is closing. The Whip linebacker is off the line in a flex position to take the cutback and help in other situations. He is playing in a 4 technique and keying the tackle. If he blocks down he is closing to his hip. We have a defensive end in a head-up alignment on the tight end with his inside arm free. That is what we call a "Jam-7 technique." We have another defensive end to the Whip side. He is interchangeable with the Whip linebacker. They can adjust their alignments according to the set we see.

For clinic talk versus the I formation both linebackers will be inside. We play a lot of man coverage. About 95 percent of the time we play man free or three-deep zone. We press the corners. We play the corners head up on the receivers in man and zone. We press them and run them back to thirds in zone. If you have three wide receivers, we have everyone on the line of scrimmage except the free safety. The free safety can be bracketed, playing in the hole or free in the middle. He can play a lot of places up and down the defense. The Whip linebacker is a defensive lineman that can run. We never bring more than five people at a time and still get great pressure on the quarterback. Just remember, who is the worst ball carrier on the football team? It is the quarterback. When he has the ball, take it away from him. Be physical with him and he will give up the ball. When we celebrate, we do it with our teammates. Never against the rules.

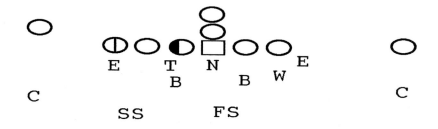

Defense is something that takes a lot of time to understand. It is simple to talk about but has a lot of complex workings in it. Our defense is a package and it is not successful when you do it just some of the time. The only people that have had any success with our defense are people that have bought into the whole defense. We are not trying to sell it. Frankly we would like it if nobody ran it. That means people are not going to understand it as well.

About the Editor

Earl Browning, the editor of the By the Experts Series, is a native of Logan, West Virginia. He currently serves as president of Telecoach, Inc.—an organization that conducts football clinics and produces the Coach of the Year Football Manuals. A 1958 graduate of Marshall University, he earned his M.Ed. and Rank I from the University of Louisville. From 1958 to 1975, he coached football at various Louisville-area high schools. Among the honors he has been accorded are his appointments to the National Football Foundations and the College Hall of Fame Advisory Committee on moving the museum to South Bend, Indiana. He was named to the Greater Louisville Football Coaches Association Hall of Legends in 1998.